Christ Jesus, The Son of Mary

A Muslim Perspective

ADIL NIZAMUDDIN IMRAN

Copyright © 2009 by Adil Nizamuddin Imran

All Rights Reserved.

Cover design by Furqaanstudios.com

The scanning, uploading and distribution of this book via the Internet or via any other means without the permission of the publisher is illegal, and punishable by law. Please purchase only authorized electronic editions, and do not participate in or encourage the electronic piracy of copyrighted materials. Your support of the author's rights is appreciated.

Publisher's Information

BOOK OF SIGNS FOUNDATION
444. E. Roosevelt Rd, Suite 173
Lombard, IL 60148

For information about special discounts or bulk purchases, please contact us at:

Phone: 888-BSF-2754 (888-273-2754)
E-mail: christjesus@bookofsigns.org
Website: www.bookofsigns.org

The views and opinions expressed in this book are expressly those of the author. They do not reflect the views and opinions of the Book of Signs Foundation.

ISBN: 978-0-9773009-5-2

PRINTED IN TURKEY

In accordance with the embodiment of servitude to the Creator, I begin with the name of God, the most compassionate, the most merciful. I also extend my most respectful salutations to Prophet Muhammad who was sent as the final messenger to all of humanity.

It is my honor to dedicate this book to my great grandfather Mir Shujauddin Hussain and my teacher Muzafar Ali Ansari, who were both spiritual masters of Hyderabad, India (may God continue to bless them both and increase their rank).

TABLE OF CONTENTS

PREFACE 1
INTRODUCTION 3
PART 1: THE BEGINNING 10
    1. Abraham, Ishmael, and the covenant 11
    2. The Coming of the Prophet 18
    3. Pillars of Islam 26
PART 2: PROPHET JESUS IN THE QURAN 46
    4. Al-Baqara (The Cow) 47
    5. Aal-E-Imran (The Family of Imran) 57
    6. An-Nisa (The Women) 89
    7. Al-Ma'idah (The Tablecloth with Food) 99
    8. Al-An'am (The Cattle) 114
    9. At-Tawba (The Repentance) 116
    10. Maryam (Mary) 118
    11. Al-Ahzab (The Coalition) 129
    12. Az-Zukhruf (The Golden Adornments) 132
    13. Al-Hadid (The Iron) 138
    14. As-Saf (The Rows) 142
PART 3: THE TRINITY AND THE CRUCIFIXION 150
    15. The Trinity 151
    16. The False Crucifixion 164
    Epilogue 170
    Appendix i
    Works Cited viii
    Suggested Readings ix

Preface

Christ Jesus The Son of Mary: A Muslim Perspective is a very well-researched and insightful book by Adil Nizamuddin Imran. The author tries to be an honest broker of information for the followers of two major faiths of the world as well as for all seekers of knowledge and truth. The easy reading style of the book has made the topics flow with such ease and harmony that the reader finds it very lucid to read, ponder and enjoy. Scholars, researchers as well as any ordinary reader from all age groups can relate to the topics of the book because of its easy language and lively presentation style. The author of this book has highlighted the person and position of Jesus Christ from an Islamic perspective with the aim of enhancing further understanding between Islam and Christianity based on knowledge, facts and mutual respect.

Throughout the ages, Christ (Peace be Upon Him) has been the center of much controversy, even within the different sects of Christianity. The Holy Bible itself testifies in its words:

"For many bare false witness against him (Jesus), but their witness agreed not together." (Mark 14:56)

The controversy about the personality of Jesus Christ is the major difference between Islam and Christianity. This difference keeps the followers of the two religions apart. Muslims look at Jesus Christ as a great Prophet of God and love and respect him as much as they love and respect Abraham, Moses and Muhammad (Peace and Blessings of the Almighty be upon All of Them).

Reverend R. Maxwell King says, "I have read in Moslem writings such deep and tender expressions of respect and reverence for Jesus that for the time I almost forgot, I was not reading the words of a Christian writer. How different, it is sad to say, has been the way in which Christians have spoken and written of Muhammad-Let us put it down to its true cause: ignorance."

But Muslims reject any divinity attributed to Christ in any form and Islam teaches that Jesus never made such a claim for himself.

On the other hand, Christians consider Jesus as God or son of God. Some of the cardinal doctrines of Christianity like the Trinity, Original Sin and Atonement are centered on it. Christians also reject the prophet hood of Muhammad (Peace be Upon Him) whom Muslims believe as God's final

Preface

messenger to all humanity until the end of time.

These two fundamental differences have often overshadowed the many similarities between Christianity and Islam. Some examples are the moral system and the emphasis on human principles. They have even over shadowed the beliefs that Muslims associate with Jesus Christ such as the Virgin Birth of Jesus, being able to speak in the cradle, performing miracles, and the second coming of Jesus Christ.

This book is a sincere and selfless effort by the author that will go a long way in building bridges of understanding, trust and brotherhood between followers of these two major faiths and help unify their ranks in serving humanity and being custodians of human morals and dignity in this age of terrible moral decay.

We fervently pray to Almighty to accept this humble effort of his, give him and his family the best reward in this world and the hereafter.

We at The Book of Signs Foundation are proud and honored to be the publisher of this precious book. We pray for complete success of the book and its mission of strengthening human brotherhood under the light of divine guidance.

Finally, we're tempted to conclude by quoting the two mighty messengers-when Christ was asked about the greatest teaching of law, his response was, "That Thy shall love Thy Lord with all thy heart, with all thy mind and with all thy soul" and Muhammad-The Prophet of Islam-when he said, "The Prophets are paternal brothers, their mothers were different but their religion is one." (Bukhari)

Blessed are the peacemakers and Peace be Upon You.

—Book of Signs Foundation

Christ Jesus, The Son of Mary: A Muslim Perspective

Introduction

In the name of Allah (God), most gracious, most merciful, these are the words that are uttered by Muslims countless times throughout the day. At the beginning of each and every action, from waking up to going to sleep, eating and drinking, putting on one's clothes, while driving, before entering and leaving home, and before commencement and completion of an action small or big. Muslims invoke the name of Almighty God not merely in religious matters but in the course of daily life. If one forgets to invoke the name of God in any action, it is believed to be lacking in some respect because it fails to acknowledge that our actions must be in harmony with the will and pleasure of God. Most readers in the Western world are unaware of the extent to which God plays a central role in the daily life of Muslims. For Muslims, Islam is a way of life that encompasses the totality of one's being. Our very existence and meaning is derived from our faith. Islam defines who we are and is the source of a Muslim's identity. Since God has created us, our primary love and devotion should reflect that reality. In fact, the word Islam in Arabic means to surrender. An additional meaning of the root word is peace. As such, Islam is the inner peace that one attains after the complete surrender to the One God. The word Muslim means the one who has surrendered and found inner peace in that surrender. Hence, everything that a Muslim does or does not do must be in consonance with what God wants of us. Some Christians may label Islam as too legalistic and rigid, but more accurately it is how Muslims are instructed to live their lives.

Most of those in the Western Hemisphere cannot comprehend the level of devotion and passion that a Muslim has for God and for Prophet Muhammad who is considered to be the final messenger sent by God to humanity. Muslims know the sacrifices that Prophet Muhammad endured so that Muslims can practice their faith in the Oneness of God. Prophet Muhammad endured severe persecution for thirteen years, which led him to leave his birth city of Mecca to Medina where he established a small Muslim community. Additionally, prior to his migration, Prophet Muhammad and his followers survived on leaves and roots after the Arab Idolaters boycotted so that no trade could be made with the Muslims. Hence, our love of God and Prophet Muhammad is immeasurable and nothing vaguely comes close to that love. Many Muslims are moved to tears at the mere mention of Prophet Muhammad's name and during recitation of the Holy

Introduction

Quran.

Failure to fully comprehend and appreciate these sentiments leads to great fissures between the Islamic world and the West. Consider the recent controversy over the publication of denigrating cartoons of Prophet Muhammad in a Danish newspaper. Millions of Muslims all over the world took to the streets to protest against this great insult. It is unfortunate that many people cannot fully grasp why something as simple as cartoons would be offensive to Muslims that would spark such an outcry. If we are a civilized and enlightened society, as the Western world claims to be, we must be respectful of these cultural orientations and religious beliefs that are considered to be so sacred. The great virtue of civility is rooted in notions of inclusiveness and tolerance of all people. From this perspective, it is fundamentally wrong to defile the sacred symbols of all religions. The cartoons were satirical and published for entertainment purposes. Consider what the Quran has to say on this subject. According to the Quran, the Holy book for Muslims, defamation of sacred symbols is strictly condemned. In Surah (the word for "chapter" in Arabic) 5:2, the Quran states **"Believers, do not violate the rites of God, or the sacred month, or the offering, or the ornaments."** Moreover, the Quran in another passage states (6:108) **"And do not insult what they pray to besides God, lest they revile God in a hostile way, without knowledge."** These verses explicitly assert that Muslims are not allowed to destroy or disrespect what other people sanctify. It is deeply unsettling as an American Muslim to watch the American flag being defiled by Muslims in other countries. This is clearly un-Islamic because the flag reflects and embodies American ideals. For this reason, all Americans by law, including Muslims, must respect the flag. By disrespecting such symbols, intolerant Muslims perpetuate negative perceptions of Muslims and Islam. The roots of the problem stem from this disconnect which prevents any meaningful dialogue between divergent faiths. Muslims for many generations have done very little in terms of interfaith dialogue and Islamic outreach in the West. In my assessment, there may be two possible explanations for this lack of Muslim initiative. The first is that Muslims today have become overly materialistic and self-absorbed. This is especially true of Muslims who migrated to the West in order to pursue greater economic opportunities. With such a mundane disposition, they purchased bigger homes and luxurious cars, sent their children to exclusive schools, and occupied themselves in worldly competition. The promotion of Islam has become the least of their concern. The second may be attributed to the fact that Western imperial powers had ruthlessly colonized the Muslim world after World War I, and indeed centuries prior. As such, Muslims have regarded Western governments as enemies while failing to separate the people from their state sanctioned foreign policies. All Muslims must learn to distinguish between foreign policy and the respective citizenry within a country. The vast majority of the people in the West are open-minded, pluralistic, and tolerant of religions. In fact, this book is dedicated to such individuals who surely will benefit from this book. To be very clear, this book is not intended to convert Christians or others to Islam. Instead, the purpose of this book is to respond to two extreme viewpoints that dominate Western perceptions of Islam.

The first perpetrators that exploit faith are the terrorists who invoke Islam and its teachings to commit vile and senseless acts of murder. An overwhelming majority of the 1.57 billion Muslims condemn suicide bombings and the killing of innocent civilians (Pew Forum). All acts of terrorism go against the principle teachings of the Quran and Prophet Muhammad. For example, it is clearly stated in a Hadith (quotations of Prophet Muhammad) that women, children, the elderly, and non-combatants are never to be attacked even during times of war. This restriction extends to trees, animals, and places of worship. Upon what basis, then, do the terrorists justify carrying out such acts of indiscriminate violence? The answer remains elusive. It has been proposed that suicide bombings are the only alternative weapons that are capable of instilling fear and causing casualties. Recall that on 9/11, fear was our initial and base emotion. People from all backgrounds and faiths came together as one collective. We were one grieving nation. However, soon afterwards, America's growing apprehension translated into an outpouring of negative emotions toward Muslims. Mosques (Muslim places of worship) were vandalized, Muslim women wearing the traditional head covering were harassed, and men with brown skin and beards began to be profiled. American Muslims were the target of hate crimes and were made to feel like strangers in their own country. America and her citizens are better than that. We should have learned from the persecution of the Native Americans, African Americans, and the internment of the Japanese during World War II. We cannot afford to repeat our previous transgressions. Any attack on America is an attack on all Americans, whether white, black, brown, Christian, Jewish, Muslim, or otherwise. Only if we stand together as one nation can we hope to defeat our common enemies. Terrorism perpetrated by Muslims has no place in Islam or any civilized society. I call on every Muslim to make their voices heard through the media and renounce any act of terrorism as a violation of the core teachings of Islam. Muslims must be more organized in getting their message so that misinformation cannot be promulgated by Christian extremists who share the other extreme viewpoint.

Introduction

After 9/11, Islam was exploited by terrorists. However, the event also crystallized fundamentalist Christians who had latent hatred for Islam and were unable to voice such beliefs due to political correctness. Religious figures such as Pat Robertson, Franklin Graham, John Haggee, Jerry Falwell, Rod Parsley, and numerous others began the open assault on Islam. Through their pulpits and Christian networks, they spread the word that Islam is an evil pagan religion, Allah is not the same God of the Bible, the Quran orders the killing of all Christian and Jewish people, and that Muslims are primitive and uncivilized people who oppress their women. All sorts of vitriolic attacks were propagated that exposed the hatred they possessed for Muslims. I apologize if I have offended those Christians who have respect for these preachers. But spreading false and odious teachings of an Abrahamic faith is not in keeping with those who claim to speak with God, or claim that even more profoundly that God speaks to them. Does their God command them to speak ill of a people who believe in Jesus Christ, his miraculous birth, the miracles he performed, his second coming, and believe he was a prophet and a man of God, believe in the Holy Spirit, who love and respect Lady Mary, Prophet Zachariah, and John the Baptist? All of these beliefs are the articles of faith for Muslims, and any deviation from these beliefs signifies a departure from Islam. In fact, the Quran specifically describes the relationship between Muslims and Christians as being close. Surah 5 verse 82 states, **"And you will certainly find the closest of them in affection to the believers are those who say, 'We are Christians.'"** Most Christians have no knowledge of the true beliefs and practices that Islam upholds. In my opinion, Muslims are more culpable for the lack of understanding that Christians have with regard to Islam than those hateful preachers. After all, Islam is the fastest growing religion in America and the West.

Muslims have a greater responsibility and obligation to teach Islam to those who have not heard its message. In Prophet Muhammad's farewell sermon, he specifically stated that those who were present should deliver the message of Islam to those who are to come. There should be a group of Muslims that invite people to Islam and promote good (see "The Farewell Sermon," in the Appendix). Islam encourages interfaith dialogue especially with those who share a common belief system and uphold a similar moral code. Unfortunately, Muslims have not engaged in dialogue with Christians. This is especially unfortunate since both faiths have the belief in Jesus Christ and Lady Mary. Of all the major religions, there is no other religion that believes in Jesus Christ except for Islam and Christianity. This includes the Jewish faith as they rejected Jesus Christ as the Messiah. On the other hand, Muslims uphold this truth as they believe that he was sent by God to teach the Scripture. This is the wonderful reality that Christians and Muslims exclusively share as part of our faiths. Hence, the purpose of this book is to begin the dialogue between Muslims and Christians by having Jesus Christ as the central figure of our discussion.

There have been many books on Islam and comparative religions written by great scholars. However, this book is different as it focuses on Jesus Christ and his family as depicted in the Quran and the Bible. The name Jesus Christ appears twenty-five times in the Quran, and this book will identify these verses and examine their meaning and significance. Through this type of inductive analysis the reader will acquire a comprehensive knowledge of the belief system espoused by Muslims. I have substantiated the Muslim position by utilizing the *New American Standard Bible*. Of the numerous versions of the Bible, I chose the *New American Standard Bible* because it is believed to be closest to the Greek translation. Although it is my understanding that Christian theologians have postulated that Jesus spoke Aramaic, and, therefore, the gospel translated from Aramaic to English would have been more accurate. However, such a translation of the original language of Jesus does not exist. All modern English versions are derived from the translation from Latin, Greek, and Hebrew.

Notwithstanding these disputes over translations and versions, what is unique is that no single entry on Jesus Christ has been added or deleted in the Quran throughout Islamic history over the span of 1,400 years. Conversely, Christian theology has evolved and developed into what exists today. Numerous ecumenical councils met to resolve various disputes concerning the identity of Jesus Christ, the Holy Spirit, and Lady Mary. In addition, when the Bible was first being compiled in the fourth century, bishops gathered to determine the makeup of the New Testament, approving the veracity of some books while rejecting others. Even today, there are differences between Protestant, Catholic, and Orthodox versions of the Bible.

It took nearly a thousand years for Christianity to fully explain the doctrine of the Trinity which remains a mystery to many. As such, I have devoted a chapter to the Trinity since it is the greatest point of disagreement between Christians and Muslims. Muslims and Jews do not uphold the triune conceptualization of God as being the Father, the Son, and the Holy Spirit. This is not consistent with the Abrahamic monotheistic tradition. However, this disagreement should not overshadow the great bond that Muslims and Christians share, and as such, a synthesis of understanding becomes possible.

Introduction

A superb example of this inclusive approach in history was the writing of St. John of Damascus in the seventh century. His critique of Islam developed in his work *On Heresy* implied that Islam was a heretical sect of Christianity. He concluded that common ground existed for the union of the two faiths. However, Islam is no more a Christian heresy than Christianity is a heresy of Judaism. In truth, the overlap of these three Abrahamic faiths is the result of the divine inspiration and revelation that the prophets proclaimed. In other words, the original source is the One true God, and therefore the three traditions embody universal teachings and share a common pedigree. Moreover, the implication that Islam is a Christian heresy insinuates that Prophet Muhammad plagiarized from the Bible. This assumption is completely erroneous because Prophet Muhammad never learned to read or write. The revelation of the Quran is the words revealed to Prophet Muhammad from the Angel Gabriel. Muslims believe all divine revelation emanated in this manner. This includes the Torah, the Ingeel (the gospel of Prophet Jesus), and the Quran. If it were the case the Prophet Muhammad took from the Bible, we would not have the specificity and details that are only found in the Quran about the lives of Mary, Jesus Christ, Zachariah, and John the Baptist. These details are not found in any Christian texts. By studying the accounts of the family of Jesus Christ in the Quran, the reader will hopefully come to understand that this is not simply a reproduction of what is found in the Bible. At the same time, there are stark differences between the two accounts. Muslims nevertheless respect both Judaism and Christianity. Muslims regard Jews and Christians as People of the Book. This gives the followers of these faiths a special status over others. For example, it is permissible for Muslim males to marry Christians and Jews. However, it is unlawful for Muslims to marry Hindus, Buddhists, atheists, and members of other faiths.

This shared bond was further illustrated during the wars between the Persians and the Christian Byzantine army in the seventh century. The Muslim Arabs would rally and cheer for the Christians to be victorious because the Persians were considered idolaters as they worshiped pagan deities. From the earliest advent of Islam, Muslims had an affinity towards Christians. Even casual observers can contrast this early Muslim sentiment with the views of St. John of Damascus and today's Christian preachers and their contempt for Islam. Preachers like Rod Parsley are quintessential examples of this growing intolerant rhetoric. In one of his sermons, Parsley proclaimed "Islam is an *antichrist* religion that intends through violence to conquer the world. America was founded, in part, with the intention of seeing this false religion destroyed." (Ross, 2008) Such people preach hate speech from the pulpit and this will invariably lead to discrimination and persecution against Muslims. To say that America was "founded to destroy this false religion" is exactly what terrorists want to hear to recruit moderate Muslims to embrace radical extremism. Islam does not teach extremism, and nor does Christianity, but it seems that both of these religions are being exploited by these fundamentalist minorities. It is up to us, Muslims and Christians, to drown out the voices of hate and come together and begin a dialogue that facilitates a greater understanding of both our religions and our people. There is far more that we share in common than the differences that divide us. The critical differences cannot be overlooked, but with a greater understanding we can learn to respectfully disagree. This is the categorical purpose of this book. It is each reader's responsibility to share this mission with others, and may each generation learn more from the ones that came before.

Part 1
The Beginning

1

Abraham, Ishmael, and the Covenant

Let us begin with how it all began. Prophet Abraham is the father of the three monotheistic traditions of Judaism, Christianity, and Islam. Islam is the continuation and culmination of the Abrahamic tradition of the worship of the One God. Islam teaches that all prophets were given this core creed to convey to their communities. Accordingly, Islam acknowledges their significance and preserves their teachings. This includes all of God's great servants like Adam, Noah, Abraham, Ishmael, Isaac, Jacob, Moses, David, Zachariah, Jesus Christ, John the Baptist, and culminating in Prophet Muhammad who is seen as the end to prophet hood. Prophet Muhammad was the only prophet from the descendants of Ishmael. As such, it becomes important to remind the reader of this narrative. In the following section we will briefly discuss Ishmael and his contributions towards the fulfillment of God's plan and prophecy. To illustrate this we will highlight the more significant passages of the Old Testament.

To begin, Ishmael was the first son of Abraham born through the concubine Hagar and the maid servant of Sarah. Although having concubines is not acceptable in today's culture, this was a rather normal practice at that time. For instance, Genesis 16: 1-2 states:

> Now Sarai, Abram's wife had borne him no children, and she had an Egyptian maid whose name was Hagar. So Sarai said to Abram, "Now behold, the Lord has prevented me from bearing children. Please go in to my maid; perhaps I will obtain children through her. And Abram listened to the voice of Sarai."

Clearly, these verses demonstrate that not only was it Sarah's idea for Abraham to have relations with Hagar, but that their offspring would astonishingly be considered children of the master Sarah. This is ironic, because it is widely believed by Jews and Christians that Ishmael is an illegitimate child and his birth is unholy. Such views are not only disrespectful to Ishmael and Hagar but also to Abraham and Sarah who were the initial actors. After all, Hagar was only being obedient to her "masters." Speaking ill about Ishmael and ignoring

Chapter 1: Abraham, Ishmael, and the Covenant

Isaac's descendants is quite disingenuous. It is documented within the Bible that four of the twelve sons of Jacob were conceived through his wives' maids. In Genesis 30:4-13, we learned that Bilah, Rachel's maid, bore Jacob two sons, Dan and Naptahli. Also Zilba, Leah's maid, bore Gad and Asher. These four sons of Jacob are not said to be illegitimate nor are they distinguished from the other eight. As Muslims we regard them highly and refer to them as the twelve sons of Jacob. However, regarding Ishmael, Muslims believe that Hagar was the wife of Abraham, thus rendering the illegitimacy argument irrelevant. This is further corroborated by Genesis 16:3, which states that "Abram's wife Sarai took Hagar the Egyptian, her maid, and gave her to her husband as his wife."

Furthermore, if we look more closely at some of the passages from the Bible concerning Ishmael and Hagar we begin to realize that they are very holy and obedient people. This is demonstrated in Genesis 16:10 - 11,

> Moreover, the angel of the Lord said to her, "I will greatly multiply your descendants so that they will be too many to count.' The angel of the Lord said to her further, 'Behold, you are with child, and you will bear a son; and you shall call his name Ishmael, because the Lord has given heed to your affliction" (Genesis 16:10-11).

These promises are also made in a similar manner to Abraham and his family.

To Abraham: Genesis 12:2 "And I will make you a great nation, and I will bless you."

To Sarah: Genesis 17:16 "I will bless her, and indeed I will give you a son by her. Then I will bless her, and she shall be a mother of nations; kings of peoples will come from her."

To Ishmael: Genesis 17:20 "As for Ishmael, I have heard you; behold; I will bless him, and will make him fruitful and will multiply him exceedingly. He shall become the father of twelve princes, and I will make him a great nation";

To Isaac: Genesis 26:24 "I am the God of your father Abraham; do not fear, for I am with you. I will bless you, and multiply your descendants, for the sake of my servant Abraham."

These passages clearly put Ishmael in a category among righteous and holy people. In fact, God praises and protects the well-being of Hagar and Ishmael when they were driven into the desert. In Genesis 21:17-20, God provided comfort and sustenance during their time of need.

> "Do not fear [Hagar], for God has heard the voice of the lad where he is. Arise, lift up the lad, and hold him by the hand, for I will make a great nation of him. Then God opened her eyes and she saw a well of water; and she went and filled the skin with water and gave the lad a drink. *God was with the lad, and he grew…*" (Genesis 21:17-20).

These verses confirm that God had a special place for Hagar and Ishmael because He was with them even though they were expelled from their home. Although Muslims have a slightly different version on the circumstances of their migration to Mecca, it is evident that their departure was part of the Divine plan. Hence, the last sentence of Genesis 16:12 states, "And he will live to the East of all his brothers." One can observe that even before Ishmael's birth, God foretold the birth of Isaac, planning for both brothers to live separately. Thus the ordeal of Hagar and Ishmael's relocation should not be viewed pejoratively as depicted in the Old Testament.

According to the Bible, it was Sarah who turned hostile towards Hagar and Ishmael claiming that their company was inappropriate for her son Isaac. Genesis 21:10 affirms "Therefore she said to Abraham, drive out this maid and her son for the son of this maid shall not be in heir with my son Isaac." This negative portrayal of Sarah does not suit her status of being not only Abraham's wife but also the mother of nations. Ironically, Muslims will defend her character and reject any suggestion of impropriety and jealousy on her part. Furthermore, the same can be said regarding the relationship between Isaac and Ishmael. The Bible implies that their relationship was adversarial and filled with jealousy, which is again not the exemplary character displayed by men of God. However, this is what we extrapolate when we read the Biblical account. It is unfortunate that the descendants of Isaac and Ishmael have over the centuries exhibited animosity and suspicion, which was not demonstrated by the immediate sons of Abraham. Quite the contrary, as both sons buried their father and both Ishmael and Isaac gave each other's children in matrimony.

One should not reveal their prejudices for their own selfish reasons by

Chapter 1: Abraham, Ishmael, and the Covenant

diminishing the honor and integrity of Ishmael in order to lift and raise the rank of Isaac. Each individual contributed differently in their own way as predetermined by God. Ishmael and Hagar's contributions to God's plan are the 1.57 billion Muslims who worship the God of Abraham and Ishmael. It is their covenant that Muslims honor and uphold. The covenant that I am referring to is found in Genesis 17:7 which states, "I will establish my covenant between me and you and your descendants after you throughout their generations for an everlasting covenant, to be God to you and your descendants after you." This verse is one of the most revealing verses that sustain the claim that Muslims follow the traditions of their forefathers. The basic principle of the covenant establishes an everlasting agreement to reaffirm God's commitment to Abraham and his descendants. Essentially, God will continue to make Him known to the descendants of Abraham in order that they worship and serve Him alone. This came to pass as God sent prophets and scriptures to various tribes and nations in order to guide them to the straight path. Concurrent to this viewpoint Muslims believe that all prophets after Abraham descended from his offspring, and as such, he is known as the "father of the prophets of God."

As a sign or seal of entering within this covenant, God required that every male be circumcised.

> "This is my covenant, which you shall keep, between me and you and your descendants after you: every male among you shall be circumcised. You shall circumcise the flesh of your foreskin, and it shall be a sign of the covenant between Me and you" (Genesis 17:10-11).

Thus, in compliance to this decree Abraham and Ishmael, and every male in his family were circumcised. Genesis 17:26 states, "In the very same day Abraham was circumcised, and Ishmael his son." This verse is significant because it suggests that not only is Ishmael included within God's covenant with Abraham but he entered that covenant on the very same day Abraham did. What is even more remarkable is that their circumcision and entrance in the covenant is nearly one year prior to the birth of Isaac. It is unfortunate that Jews and Christians completely ignore this fact. They vehemently oppose any notion that Ishmael and his descendants, namely Arabs and Muslims, have any covenant with God. They contend that Isaac and his descendants are the only people who have God's covenant conferred upon them. To validate this claim they cite Genesis 17:19-21 which states:

God said "No, but Sarah your wife shall bear you a son, and you shall call his name Isaac; and I will establish My covenant with him as an everlasting covenant for his descendants after him. But my covenant, I will establish with Isaac whom Sarah will bear to you at this season next year" (19-20).

These verses clearly suggest that Isaac and not Ishmael had been chosen by God to keep and maintain the covenant. Ostensibly, there does appear a contradiction between Genesis 17:7 and 17:21. Certainly, God did not require Ishmael and every male in Abraham's household to be circumcised needlessly. This being said, how then can we explain this inconsistency? It is obvious that God can make a covenant or agreement with anyone or anything and it need not be exclusive. For example, in Genesis 6:18 God makes a covenant with Noah, "But I shall establish my covenant with you; and you shall enter the ark." Therefore, one can reasonably believe God can and does have more than one covenant without there appearing to be any contradiction.

It is clear that there is no contradiction between the covenant Ishmael entered in Genesis 17:7 and Isaac's exclusive covenant in Genesis 17:21. In essence, the covenant made with Isaac is simply another more specific covenant in which God selected Isaac to establish a community that would be exclusively founded on God's laws. This does not, however, abrogate the covenant of Genesis 17:7 which Ishmael and his descendants entered into to worship the One God. Isaac not only shares in the covenant made in Genesis 17:7 but he had a special covenant with God in Genesis 17:21. Isaac's covenant came to fruition when God chose his descendants, mainly the Sons of Jacob, who received guidance and scriptures through numerous prophets, more so than any other community. God's commitment was honored from the time of Abraham to the time of Jesus who was the last prophet sent to the Sons of Jacob until the covenant was broken by them. The Bible states:

"My covenant which they broke, although I was a husband to them" (Jeremiah 31:32).

Thus says the Lord, "If you can break My covenant for the day and My covenant for the night, so that day and night will not be at their appointed time, then My covenant may also be broken with David My servant so that he will not have a son to reign on his throne, and with Levitical priests, My ministers"

Chapter 1: Abraham, Ishmael, and the Covenant

(Jeremiah 33:20-21).

We read throughout the Bible countless egregious sins committed by the descendants of Jacob including killing prophets, idol worship, manipulating scriptures, disobedience of the law, and so forth. This inevitably led God to break his covenant with the Jewish people. Muslims believe the turning point occurred when the Jews sought to crucify Jesus, their Messiah, who was sent to save the House of Israel. "For he shall save his people from their sins" (Matthew 1:24). However, their pride led most of them to deny Jesus' prophet hood and his Gospel, resulting in their old practice of murdering men of God.

The reader may find such a line of reasoning to be harsh, but reality in this case cannot be avoided. In matters of truth, one must speak the truth. Since Prophet Jesus was sent as the final prophet to the House of Israel, God in his infinite mercy sent the prophet to the Gentiles, namely the descendants of Ishmael. In the following section, I will highlight and examine the relevant Biblical passages that foretold the coming of the Prophet to and from the Gentiles.

Before I document the coming of the prophet (Prophet Muhammad) let us first recapitulate what we have gathered about Ishmael since Prophet Muhammad is the only prophet who was his direct descendant.

1. Ishmael entered into God's covenant with Abraham (Genesis 17:7)

2. God was with "the lad" as he grew (Genesis 21:20)

3. Ishmael settled in the land of the East. But to the sons of his concubines, Abraham gave gifts while he was still living and sent them away from his son Isaac Eastward, to the Land of the East. (Genesis 25:6)

4. God will make Ishmael a great nation (Genesis 17:20)

A great nation implies that Ishmael and his descendants will be godly, because they must abide by the covenant that they serve and worship the One and only God. Once they strayed from this path and began to worship other gods, then it becomes necessary to send a prophet to bring them back to the worship of the One and only true God. This was the exclusive purpose for which prophets were sent.

"Yet He sent prophets to them to bring them back to the Lord" (2nd Chronicles 24:19).

Therefore, to maintain the covenant with Ishmael, God sent Prophet Muhammad to the Gentile Arabs who were engaged in idol worship along with other transgressions in pre-Islamic Arabia. Prophet Muhammad's coming is prophesied in many verses of the Bible. The next chapter is devoted to an analysis of these passages.

2

The Coming of the Prophet

According to the Quran, Prophet Muhammad's coming was foreshadowed by earlier prophets and their scriptures. Surah 7:157 states**, "Those who follow the messenger, the unlettered prophet of whom they find written in their sources, in the Torah and the Gospel. He directs them to what is just and forbids them from evil. And he permits them wholesome things and forbids them filthy things. He removes their burden for them, and the yokes that were on them."** This verse is explicitly clear that the earlier divine scriptures foretold the coming of the Prophet Muhammad. Hence, in this chapter let us highlight those passages in the Bible that refer to the coming of the prophet, Prophet Muhammad.

First, we read in John 1:19-21:

This is the testimony of John, when the Jews sent to him priests and Levites from Jerusalem to ask him, "Who are you?" And he confessed and did not deny, but confessed, "I'm not the Christ." They asked him, "What then? Are you Elijah?" And he said "I am not." "Are you the Prophet?" And he answered, "No".

From this conversation between John the Baptist and Jewish priests, we learn that the Jews are awaiting the coming of three distinct people: the Christ, Elijah, and the Prophet. We now know that Jesus was the Christ and Messiah whom the Jews denied but the Muslims later affirmed. This leaves Elijah and the Prophet. With respect to Elijah, it is believed by Jews and some Christians that he has not yet returned but will do so to announce the Second Coming of Jesus Christ.

Thus, we need to account for The Prophet. Even today the Jews are still awaiting his arrival and the Christians believe Jesus Christ was the Prophet. This latter assertion of Christians is impossible because it is clear from John 1:21 as well as John 1:25 that "The Prophet" is a separate and distinct person from Elijah and the Christ. John 1:25 states "Why then are you, John the Baptist, baptizing, if you are not the Christ, nor Elijah, nor the Prophet?" The questioning priests were trying to identify whether John the Baptist was one of these three individuals. The knowledge of the coming of these three was known not only by Jewish priests but also ordinary Jews. This is supported by John 7:40-41 which clearly identifies the distinction that Jewish people are making with regard to Jesus of Nazareth. John 7:40-41 states, "Some of the people, therefore, when they heard these words were saying this certainly is the Prophet. Others were saying, 'This is the Christ.'" Hence, we can reasonably assert that the Prophet and the Christ are two separate and distinct men of God.

We know that Jesus Christ was a prophet, just as John the Baptist was. On the other hand, Muslims claim that Prophet Muhammad was *the* Prophet that Jews were asking about in the above passage. In fact, in the entire Quran, which is longer than both the Torah and the New Testament, the name "Muhammad" appears only four times. God addresses Prophet Muhammad as "the Prophet" or "the Messenger". However, the Jews came to deny his prophet hood when they learned that he was the descendant of Ishmael and a non-Jew. Obviously, this is not a valid reason to reject any prophet of God, let alone *the* Prophet. The fact is that the Jews believed then and even today that they alone are God's chosen people. If such a claim were true, what would have happened to all the Gentiles who had not received divine guidance, especially the descendants of Ishmael as they had a covenant with God? We as Muslims believe that it would be an act of injustice if God had exclusively sent guidance to Jews while neglecting other communities.

Moreover, it was prophesied that there would come a time when **the** prophet would be passed from Judah and the Children of Israel to another community.

In Isaiah 3:1-2, it states:

"For behold, the Lord God of hosts is going to remove from Jerusalem and Judah both supply and support, the whole supply of bread and the whole supply of water; the mighty man and the warrior, the judge and the prophet..."

This passage clearly asserts that God will take away from Judah and Jerusalem the Judge and the Prophet. Hence, if he (the Prophet) is to come, he must be from outside Jerusalem and not from the tribe of Judah. We know that Prophet Muhammad is from the descendants of Ishmael and he was born in Mecca.

Another explicit validation that foreshadows the coming of Prophet Muhammad is found in Genesis 49:10. It states, "The *scepter shall not depart* from Judah, nor the rulers staff from between his feet, *until Shiloh comes*, and to him shall be the obedience of the peoples." Although the verse is very clear, let us provide some perspective. Before his death, Jacob gathered his twelve sons and told them what each one would face in the coming days. In this verse, Jacob addresses Judah who is the lawgiver which is confirmed in the statement "and Judah is my scepter or lawgiver" (Psalms 60:7). As such, in Genesis 49:10, Jacob informs Judah that in the future the scepter will pass from him to Shiloh. The question is: who is Shiloh?

Christians believe that Shiloh refers to Jesus Christ. However, this verse cannot be in reference to Christ because the scepter was to *depart from Judah* and go to Shiloh. Jesus is a direct descendant of Judah (Matthew 1), and therefore he cannot be Shiloh. In other words, Shiloh will possess the scepter and will be the lawgiver, and he will not be from Judah. Additionally, the notion that Jesus Christ was Shiloh and the lawgiver can be refuted when we consider that according to Christian doctrine Jesus did not produce any new law and nor did he claim to be the lawgiver. If we believe the testimony of both Apostles Peter and Paul, they were inspired to revoke the erstwhile Jewish law and taught that Christians no longer needed to abide by such doctrines. However, 49:10 makes complete sense when we consider Prophet Muhammad as Shiloh since he brought forth a new law in the Quran. This is consistent with Isaiah 3:1-2, whereby God will remove from Judah the judge and the prophet. Here, the judge and the prophet refer to the scepter or lawgiver. These three passages – John 1:21, Genesis 49:10, and Isaiah 3:1 – validate the truthfulness of Prophet Muhammad as a prophet and messenger of God.

There is another passage that is quite comprehensive and it is found in Isaiah 46:10-11:

"Declaring the end from the beginning, from ancient times

things which have not been done, Saying 'My purpose will be established and I will accomplish all My good pleasure'; Calling a bird of prey from the east, the man of My purpose from a far country. Truly I have spoken; truly I will bring it to pass. I have planned it, surely I will do it." (Isaiah 46:10-11).

Some Old Testament commentaries, such as *Wesley's Notes* and *Geneva Study Bible*, refer to "the man of my purpose" as being Cyrus the Great. But this is erroneous because Cyrus is nowhere identified as a prophet or a man of God. Instead, it is believed he was an idol worshipper and an unbeliever. If God since the beginning had chosen him for a purpose, he would have needed to demonstrate that he was a faithful and obedient servant. Yet his primary contribution was to give the Jews permission to rebuild the Temple. King Solomon built the Temple in 957 BC and King Nebuchadnezzar destroyed it in 587 BC. Again, it was rebuilt by revered prophets such as Zachariah and Ezra in 515 BC with Cyrus' permission and, later in 40 BC, Herod the Great expanded the Temple.

On the other hand, Isaiah 46:10-11 accurately describes the Muslim position of Prophet Muhammad's coming. In verse 10, we learn that God had declared the end from the beginning implying the sending of prophets. An important belief of Muslims is that Prophet Muhammad as the final prophet of God was conveyed to Adam, the first human creation and prophet. We know from verse 11 that God is referring to "the man of my purpose" (prophet) and he will be the final end to prophet hood. Also in verse 10 we are told that God had not done whatever he planned since ancient times. This too is revealing because since the time of Ishmael, there had not been a single prophet sent to his descendants in nearly 2500 years.

Moreover, Prophet Muhammad was the only prophet from the descendants of Ishmael and he was a prophet for all peoples. Genesis 49:10 ends with the following, "To him shall be the obedience of the peoples." God sending a single prophet for all the peoples had not been done since Noah's time. Noah was a prophet to all the people and when his people rejected God and continued in their sins, God destroyed them and all creatures in the flood. The only survivors were Noah and his family. "The sons of Noah and Noah's wife and the three wives of his sons with them, entered the Ark" (Genesis 7:13). If there were any other prophets living at that time, then God would have saved them as well. Thus, we can reasonably assume that Noah was the only prophet to all the peoples of the Earth. Since Noah, God had not sent a prophet to all the peoples. Such was the

Chapter 2: The Coming of the Prophet

case until Prophet Muhammad.

Also, we learn from verse 11 that the man of God will come from a far country of the east. Again, this is consistent with Prophet Muhammad who was born in Mecca where his forefathers settled over 2500 years earlier. If you recall, it was foretold that Ishmael would live "east of his brothers" in Genesis 16:12 and in Genesis 25:6 we see that Abraham sent Ishmael eastward to settle in the "land of the east." Taken together, these specific verses refer to Prophet Muhammad and no one else. This should not come as a surprise to Jews and Christians because God is not just the Lord of them exclusively. Rather, He is the One true God revealed to Prophet Muhammad and worshiped by Muslims.

Since we have demonstrated the necessity and truthfulness of Prophet Muhammad using Biblical text, let us ponder over a few more passages that will further corroborate the veracity of Prophet Muhammad as the prophet of and for the Gentiles. There are two clear passages that convey the shift to the Gentiles and the completion of God's revelation and guidance only to the Sons of Jacob. The first is found in Isaiah 42:1, "Behold, My Servant, whom I uphold; My chosen one in whom my soul delights. I have put My Spirit upon Him; He will bring forth justice to the nations." In the Bible, 'nations' is used in reference to Gentiles. This verse is clear that God will choose a prophet or servant who will bring justice to all nations or Gentiles. The question again arises: who was this chosen servant or prophet?

According to the Gospel of Matthew, Jesus was the servant referred to by Isaiah. In Matthew 12:18, it states,

> "Behold, My Servant whom I have chosen; My Beloved in whom My soul is well-pleased; I will put My Spirit upon Him, and He shall proclaim justice to the Gentiles" (Matthew 12:18).

Although Matthew is a revered Apostle, I believe that he erroneously interpreted this verse in Isaiah as referring to Jesus. It is very clear that Jesus Christ did not ever preach, let alone proclaim justice, to the Gentiles. In the Gospels, there is not a single documented testimony of Jesus in which he preached to the Gentiles and nor was he sent for their salvation. In fact, quite the opposite was true. He would avoid dealing with any Gentiles and in Matthew 15:26 he referred to the Gentiles as dogs. It says, "And he answered and said, "It is not good to take the children's bread and throw it to the dogs."

Although this verse seems pejorative and portrays Jesus negatively, Muslims regard him to be a steadfast devotee of God and a prophet of character worthy of emulation. Here, the point simply is that Jesus was not sent to the Gentiles but to the Jewish people, as he articulated in many verses. For example, in Matthew 1:21 Jesus' purpose and goal is stated prior to his birth.

> "She [Mary] will bear a son and you shall call His name Jesus for He shall save *His people* from their sins" (Matthew 1:21).

Also, in Matthew 5:17, Jesus said

> "Do not think I came to abolish the Law of the Prophets; I did not come to abolish but to fulfill" (Matthew 5:17).

These verses clearly state that not only was he sent to the Jews but his mission was to preserve the Law of Moses and not to usurp it. Recall that the law does not apply to the Gentiles. But the most compelling verse in this regard is to be found in Matthew 15:24 which states "I was sent only to the lost sheep of the House of Israel." After contemplating these verses, it is specious to suggest that Isaiah 42:1 can be interpreted as applying to Jesus Christ.

Furthermore, not only did Jesus refrain from preaching to the Gentiles but he forbade his disciples not to go near the Gentiles. In Matthew 10:5-6 we read,

> These twelve Jesus sent out after instructing them; "Do not go in the way of the Gentiles, and do not enter any city of the Samaritans; but rather go to the lost sheep of the house of Israel."

Thus, the disciples continued to preach solely to the Jews many years after Jesus Christ's ascension into heaven as stated in the following verse "speaking the word to no one except to Jews alone" (Acts 11:19).

Let's not ignore the fact that he was called "King of the Jews." The Bible says "So Pilate asked Him, saying, 'are you the King of the Jews?' And He answered him and said, 'It is as you say'" (Luke 23:3). Considering all these factual proofs, Matthew's interpretation that Jesus was the chosen servant is not correct. This then questions the Gospel's infallibility. Again, concerning Isaiah 42:1, I believe that a stronger case can be made for Prophet Muhammad as being

Chapter 2: The Coming of the Prophet

the chosen servant who would proclaim justice to the Gentiles. Also, it should be understood that Prophet Muhammad was an Arab and the Arabs are the descendants of Ishmael. As such, they are more entitled to divine guidance than the Gentiles within Paul's ministry. It was Paul of Tarsus who, after persecuting Christians, became a believer and began to preach his own doctrine. He did away with the Law of Moses and he replaced it with the death, burial, resurrection and redemption doctrine. He was also the main proponent of preaching to the Gentiles which directly contradicted the teachings of Jesus Christ and the original Apostles. However, Ishmael's descendants, who are Gentiles, previously had a covenant with God. Neither the Greeks nor the Romans had any covenant with God as the one made with Abraham and his sons Ishmael and Isaac. As such, it is reasonable to presume that God did send a Gentile prophet to the Arab Gentiles so that they may embrace God's laws and commandments.

A final passage for consideration suggesting the transfer of divine guidance from the Jewish people is found in Matthew 21:43. It states, "Therefore, I say to you, that the Kingdom of God will be taken away from you and given to a people producing the fruit of it." This verse is very clear that the Jewish people will no longer have the Kingdom of God. They will no longer reign and another faithful community will emerge. The obvious question is: who are "a people" that Jesus Christ is speaking of who will bear the fruits? Clearly, it cannot be the Jewish people because Jesus Christ is speaking to the Jews when he stated "the Kingdom of God will be taken away from you." This leaves the Gentile world. Christians may believe that they are the people that Jesus Christ is referring to in Matthew 21:43 to whom the Kingdom of God was given. To accept this however, we would have to ignore the history of first century Christians who were predominately Jewish. Were these people not part of the Kingdom of God?

In my assessment after careful analysis, the people that were given "the Kingdom of God, producing the fruit of it" were the Muslim Gentiles. To reiterate my earlier point, if God were going to intervene by sending a prophet to a people other than the Sons of Jacob, it would have to be to the descendants of Ishmael for they are the descendants of Abraham with whom God established a covenant. He did not have any such covenant with the Greeks, Romans, or any other Gentile nation but with Ishmael from whom God promised "a great nation." Hence, Muslims believe Prophet Muhammad was sent to maintain God's covenant and fulfill the divine plan. Prior to Islam in the seventh century, pre-Islamic Arabia was known as the "age of ignorance." The Arab pagans of the time were engaged in idol worship, tribal warfare, female infanticide, and took advantage of the rights of orphans and the poor. It is in this atmosphere that Prophet Muhammad was sent to bring people back to the path of God. In the next chapter, let us examine the core beliefs and pillars of the Islamic faith.

3
Pillars of Islam

In this section we will discuss the foundations of Islam, which are built upon the five pillars each Muslim is obligated to practice. The five pillars are as follows:

1. Shahadah, or Declaration of Faith

2. Five daily prayers (Salah)

3. Fasting in the month of Ramadan

4. Tithing (Zakat), totaling 2.5% of savings

5. Hajj, or pilgrimage to Mecca

Let us now examine each one of the pillars in greater detail, starting with the first.

PILLAR ONE: SHAHADAH (DECLARATION OF FAITH)

"For your God is one God; there is no deity besides the Benevolent, the Merciful." (Surah 2:163)

The Shahadah, which means "witness" in Arabic, is the first and most important pillar in that it requires the individual to recognize and believe that there is no God but God and Prophet Muhammad is the Messenger of God. By this declaration, a person has entered Islam, thereby becoming a Muslim. A myriad of books have been written which discuss Prophet Muhammad. For example, Martin Lings, author of *Muhammad: His Life Based on the Earliest*

Christ Jesus, The Son of Mary: A Muslim Perspective

Sources, is an excellent text with which to study the life of the Prophet. However, for our purposes, let us focus our attention on a brief overview of the Muslim conceptualization of God.

Just as a note, Allah is the name of God, as is Jehovah or Yaweh in the Old Testament. Allah is not a pronoun, and in my opinion, should not be translated as a general term for God.

More important is the effort by some Christians and Jews to claim that Jehovah is the Hebrew name of God, but Allah and Jehovah are not one and the same. This dispute promulgated by ignorant Christian scholars reminds me of the similar effort of Marcion and his followers. Marcion, a second century priest, taught his Christian followers that the God of the Old Testament is not the God of the New Testament. He believed that the God of the Jews and the Old Testament was an angry, jealous, and hateful God. But the God of the Christians and New Testament was a kind, loving and merciful God (Gonzalez, 1984). This specious proposition must have been confusing to the early Jews, given that Jesus Christ was Jewish, and sent to preach to the Jews in their synagogues. Marcion may have believed this distance from the Jewish faith would be socially and politically advantageous, because they were perceived as rebels within the Roman Empire after their failed attempt at reclaiming Jerusalem in 65 A.D. It seems as though Marcion did to the Jews what Christians are doing to the Muslims. Some preachers are promulgating a similar message post 9/11, distancing the God of Christians from the God of Muslims. However, today we would laugh at Marcion for such a decree, and I hope that after reading the next section you will do the same.

To add to the confusion, some Christians have promulgated the belief that Allah was the pagan god the Arabs worshipped. Prior to Prophet Muhammad, the worship of one God had been lost by the descendants of Ishmael. The Arabs, like the sons of Jacob, had at one point in their history begun to worship idols. They had over 360 idols housed in the Kabba, which was built by Abraham and Ishmael. What is interesting about the 360 idols is that the Arabs contended that Allah was the invisible God, creator of the Universe, and above all the others. They were correct in their belief in Allah, but they had lost sight of His oneness, which had been reintroduced by Prophet Muhammad. Prophet Muhammad was against any form of idol worship. In fact, the first moment he entered into the Kabba, having won Mecca without a battle, he destroyed all 360 idols. Moreover, some Christians claim that Allah is the "moon god" because of the symbolism of the moon and stars on the flags of some Muslim countries. This, too, is erroneous. There are numerous verses in the Quran that reveal the purpose of why the moon was created. It is used as a calendar and is a beautiful torch to guide travelers. In Surah 10, verse 5 it states, **"It is God who has made the sun shine and the moon glow, and determined lunar phases that you may know the number of the years, and the calculation. God did not create that in any way but right; God makes these signs clear to people who discern."** That being said, let me return to answering the more important question: how do Muslims conceptualize the one and almighty God, Allah?

There are many scholars who have written on this topic, but the one I find to be the most concise and comprehensive is the twelfth century scholar Imam Ghazali. Below follows an excerpt from his text, *The Revival of the Religious Sciences*:

> "God in His essence is One, without any partner, Single without any similar, Eternal without any opposite, Separate without any like. He is One: prior with nothing before Him, from eternity, without any beginning, abiding in existence with none after Him, in Eternity, without any end, subsisting without ending, abiding without termination. He hath not ceased, and He will not cease to be described with glorious epithets. He is the First and Last, the External and Internal and He knows everything.
>
> We witness that He is not a body possessing bounds and limits—He does not resemble bodies either in limitation or in accepting division. He is not a substance, no entity resembles him, nothing is like Him and He is not like anything, measure does not limit Him and boundaries do not contain Him, the directions do not surround Him and neither the earth nor heavens are on different sides of Him.
>
> There is not in His essence his equal, nor in His equal His essence. He is far removed from change of state or of place. Events have no place in Him and mishaps do not befall Him. Nay, He does not cease through His glorious qualities to be far removed from changing and through His perfect qualities to be independent of perfecting increase.

We witness that He is living, powerful and commanding. Inadequacy and weakness befall Him not, He is the Lord of the Worlds—the visible world and the invisible, that of force and that of might, He possesses rule, creation and the command: He created the creatures and their works and decreed their sustenance and their terms of life.

We witness that He knows all the things that can be known, comprehending that which happened from the bounds of the earth unto the highest heavens; no grain in the earth or in the heavens is distant from His knowledge—yes, He knows the creeping of the little ant upon the rugged rock in a dark night and He perceives the movement of the mote in the midst of the air; He knows the secret and the concealed and has knowledge of the suggestions of the minds and the movement of the thoughts and the concealed things of the inmost parts—by a knowledge which is prior from eternity.

We witness that He is The Willer of the things that are, and the things that happen; there does not come about in the world, seen or unseen, little or much, small or great, good or evil, advantage or disadvantage, faith or unbelief, knowledge or ignorance, success or loss, increase or diminution, obedience or rebellion—except by His will. What He wills happens, and what He doesn't will doesn't happen. Not a glance of one who looks, or a slip of one who thinks is outside His will; He is the Creator, the Resurrecter, the Doer of that which He wills.

And we witness that He is the All Hearing, the All Seeing and no audible thing is distant from His hearing and no visible thing is far from His seeing, however fine it may be. Distance does not curtain off His hearing and darkness does not dull His seeing.

And we witness that He speaks, commands, forbids, praises as well as threatens with a speech that is subsisting in His essence from all eternity, not resembling the speech of created things. He is Living, Knowing, Powerful, Willer,

Hearer, Seer as well as Speaker through Life. Power, Knowledge, Will, Hearing, Seeing, Speech—none of these are separated from His essence."

SECOND PILLAR: SALAH (FIVE DAILY PRAYERS)

"And seek help by patience and prayer, though that is formidable but for the humble." (Surah 2:45)

The second pillar of Islam is the five daily prayers, called Salah, and is required by every Muslim from the time of puberty. The prayers (Salah) are spread throughout the day as a reminder to Muslims of their true purpose in life, which is the obedience and worship of God. The first prayer, called Fajr is performed at dawn an hour or so before sunrise. The second prayer, Dhuhr is done in the afternoon shortly after the sun reaches its zenith. The third prayer, Asr is performed in the mid afternoon around 1 ½ hours before sunset. The fourth prayer, called Maghrib is performed immediately after sunset. The fifth prayer, Isha'a, is performed at night. These are the fixed times that Muslims throughout the world follow. Fortunately, in the Muslim countries and in places with a large Muslim population there is a designated person, known as the Muezzin, who calls the Muslims to prayer. This is similar to the Christian usage of bells and the Jewish horn to signify the time of worship.

Since the Quran was revealed in Arabic, and the Salah is a recitation of the Quran, it is necessary for Muslims to learn to read Arabic as well as memorize portions of the Quran. The requirement of memorizing the Quran is a great blessing for Muslims in that it the means by which the Quran is preserved. It has been over 1400 years since the Quran was revealed to Prophet Muhammad, and to this day the Quran maintains its authenticity without any corruption. Despite it containing 114 chapters and over 6236 verses, there are millions of Muslims who have memorized the entire Quran in its original Arabic text. Some children as young as six years old have completed this monumental task despite the fact that Arabic may not be their native language. Muslims believe that this is proof of the Quran's status as a divine work, as it resides in the hearts of people. This example of complete memorization of scripture in its original text is not replicated by any other religion or its respective scripture.

The prayers themselves are very short and simple. They usually take 5 to 10 minutes. However, before the prayer is made, there is a ritual washing (ablution) of the hands, mouth, face, arms, and feet called *wudu*. This is done so that when an individual is in the presence of God and worshipping him, they are physically pure. It should be noted that cleanliness is a part of all faiths, especially the Abrahamic religions. Like Muslims, the Jews had an extensive tradition of physical purity and cleanliness. Moreover, the Christians had an area built inside the cathedrals for ritual washing before they entered the main worship area.

After the ritual washing is performed, Muslims are ready to stand before God and offer Salah (prayer). Now, let me highlight a few points regarding these prayers. An important aspect of the prayers is humbling oneself by prostrating before the Creator. This gesture, placing one's face on the ground, is well documented in the previous scriptures. This was done by Abraham in Genesis 17:3 ("Abraham fell on his face, and God talked with him…,"), by Moses in Numbers 14:5 ("Then Moses and Aaron fell on their faces in the presence of all the assembly of the congregation of the sons of Israel.") and by Jesus in Matthew 26:39 ("And He went a little beyond them, and fell on His face and prayed."). Muslims also have been taught by Prophet Muhammad to prostrate within the prayer because the servant is closest to God while prostrating.

Another significant aspect of the prayer that may be interesting to Christians appears at the end of the prayer. At the end of each prayer, Muslims recite, "O God, bless Muhammad and the people of Muhammad; as you have blessed Abraham and the people of Abraham. Surely you are Praiseworthy, the Glorious. O God, be gracious unto Muhammad and the people of Muhammad; as you were gracious unto Abraham and the people of Abraham. Surely you are Praiseworthy, the Glorious." Moreover, there are numerous prayers in which Muslims send their blessings and peace upon Abraham and all the other Prophets. Such prayers demonstrate that Islam is the religion that affirms the earlier prophets and embraces their traditions. For this reason, God has blessed Muslims as he promised to do in Genesis, "I will bless those who bless you, and the one who curses you I will curse" (Genesis 12:3).

Outside of the five daily prayers, there is a special prayer each Friday. The Friday prayer, known as the Juma prayer is especially significant because it is done in large congregations. Muslims are required to make this prayer in their local mosque, which is the Muslim place of worship, comparable to a church or synagogue. Congregational prayer is important as it creates a sense of community and forms stronger bonds between fellow Muslims.

Chapter 3: Pillars of Islam

The prayer itself includes a short ten/fifteen minute sermon led by an Imam, the spiritual leader of a mosque. After the sermon, the Imam leads the congregation in a short prayer. The entire event spans no more than thirty minutes. Upon completion, Muslims are encouraged to be social with one another, but are otherwise free to resume their daily routine- unlike the Jewish and Catholic traditions, which impose restrictions against working and other remedial tasks during the Sabbath. Friday is a holy day, but there are no undue prohibitions attached to it. After the Friday prayer, Muslims go about their business like any other day. Friday was chosen as the holy day because it was on Friday (the sixth day) that Prophet Adam was created, and to honor his memory, Muslims celebrate Friday as the holy day, since we are descendants of Adam.

Let me briefly mention the setup of the prayers in mosques. There is an Imam at the front of the congregation, followed by the men and then the women. This construction is not based upon the superiority of men over women, as presumed by non-Muslims, but the genders are segregated so that there is no temptation that can interfere in the worship. It is exclusively for this reason that Islam segregates the genders and encourages certain boundaries between them. It sounds very primitive, but it is very effective, and problems that arise when there is free and open interaction between the sexes are not found in the Muslim world, such as preteen/teen premarital sex, adultery, children born out of wedlock and rape.

For this reason, there are strict guidelines in place regarding the attire of both men and women. The Quran states in 24:30: **"Say to the believing men that they should lower their gaze and guard their modesty: that will make for greater purity for them: And God is well acquainted with all that they do."** In this verse, God addresses the men first and orders them to lower their gaze and not seek out temptation. In the subsequent verse, God addresses the women: **"And say to the believing women that they should lower their gaze and guard their modesty; that they should not display their beauty and ornaments except what (must ordinarily) appear thereof; that they should draw their veil over their bosoms and not display their beauty..."** (Surah 24:31) This verse has been interpreted as requiring Muslim women to cover their adornments- including the hair, but not the face. The *niqab,* or face veil, is a conservative interpretation by scholars, though the majority do not require it and its use is not widespread in the Muslim world. Along with the head covering, they should dress in loose clothing so as not to reveal their figures or invite salacious thoughts towards them by onlookers. The head covering is meant as a protection from sin.

As stated in Mark 9:47, Jesus Christ cautions against temptations of the eye that lead to sin. "And if your eye causes you to sin, pluck it out. It is better for you to enter the kingdom of God with one eye than to have two eyes and be thrown into hell". Hence, for both men and women, the veil facilitates harmonious social order. Although from a Western perspective the head covering is a sign of women's subjugation by men, this notion is frankly, nonsense. This is evident by the conversion of women in the West, who choose to wear the head covering to adhere to the teaching of the Quran. Some of these women are modern, educated, and working women who are not in any way dominated by men. They are simply following the Abrahamic traditions. In the New Testament, the following statement is made by St. Paul, "If a woman does not cover her head, she should have her hair cut off; and if it is a disgrace for a woman to have her hair cut off or shaved off, she should cover her head" (1 Corinthians 11). Again, the head covering is a sign of humility and conceals the beauty of the woman from onlookers, and protects her from ill thoughts. The hijab that a Muslim woman wears is no different than what a nun wears, and one ordinarily should not have any ill thoughts when they see a nun in her habit. It is in keeping with Jewish and early Christian traditions and has been adopted by Muslims for both their prayers and daily lives.

THIRD PILLAR: FASTING IN THE MONTH OF RAMADAN

"O believers, fasting is prescribed for you, as it was prescribed for those before you, that you may be conscientious." (Surah 2:183)

The Third Pillar of Islam is fasting in the month of Ramadan, which every Muslim who has reached puberty is required to partake in. Ramadan is the ninth month in the Muslim calendar, and contains the day in which the Quran was first revealed to Prophet Muhammad. Before we begin our discussion about fasting, I think it would be appropriate to mention at this time a few things about the Quran. The Quran is not the word of Prophet Muhammad but the Word of God brought by Angel Gabriel. Prophet Muhammad's companions were able to differentiate the Quranic text from the sayings of the Prophet, known as the Hadiths. Thus, when people unfamiliar with the Islamic faith say that the Quran is the word of Prophet Muhammad, they are mistaken. No Muslim believes that the Quran is the word of the Prophet, as he was unable to read or write. Prophet Muhammad received God's revelation, the Quran, just as all prophets received revelation, including Moses, the recipient of the Torah; David, the recipient of the Zaboor (the Psalms), and Jesus, the recipient of the Ingeel (the Gospel).

Chapter 3: Pillars of Islam

The Quran does not follow a chronological pattern so that the early revelations of the Quran do not necessarily appear in the beginning of the book. The text is laid out exactly how Angel Gabriel instructed Prophet Muhammad. However, we know precisely when and where each Surah was revealed, and under what circumstances, so that the Quran can be written chronologically. The Quran was preserved by numerous companions of Prophet Muhammad who had put it to memory but also committed it to writing. However, that which was written had not been put into a book form. Rather, the entire transcript of the Quran was loosely assembled. Not only was there a scarcity in ink and paper, there were even fewer people who knew how to read or write. Like Prophet Muhammad the majority of Arabs did not learn to read or write, simply because it was not seen as necessary for survival. As such, the oral tradition was the most common means of preserving knowledge. For those few who were capable of reading and writing, Prophet Muhammad assigned them the task of transcribing the Quran as it was being revealed. Furthermore, in each Ramadan, Angel Gabriel would hear the Prophet reciting the Quran as a review. In fact, during the Prophet's last Ramadan, Angel Gabriel heard him recite the Quran twice in its entirety. Thus, when it came to putting the Quran into book form, the companions of the Prophet utilized both the written and oral testimony, as there were many followers who had committed the Quran to memory. This should not seem unusual, as in Jeremiah 31:33, God has promised that law is to be preserved in the minds and hearts of the Jewish people. "'But this is the covenant which I will make with the house of Israel after those days,' declares the Lord, 'I will put My law within them and on their heart I will write it; and I will be their God, and they shall be My people.'" However, Muslims have demonstrated that God's promise can be fulfilled, as they have preserved the Quran in its entirety in their hearts and minds. Hence, if the written record of the Quran is altered or lost, there are millions of Muslims who can reproduce it in the original Arabic text. What is most remarkable about the Prophet's first revelation by the Angel Gabriel is that it is quite similar to what is found in Isaiah 29:12. "Then the book will be given to the one who is illiterate, saying, "Please read this." And he will say, "I cannot read.""

Prophet Muhammad was illiterate- his entire life he never learned to read or write. While praying one day in the cave of Hiraa, the Angel Gabriel appeared to the Prophet suddenly, and ordered him to "Iqra!" (read, recite, repeat, proclaim). Prophet Muhammad, in his terror thought he was being asked to read, so he stammered: "I am unlettered." The Angel Gabriel again ordered him to "Iqra!" and again he replied, "I am unlettered." The Angel Gabriel now took a firm hold of him and commanded him "Iqra in the name of God who created!"

Now Prophet Muhammad began to understand that he was not being asked to read, but to recite, or repeat. He began to repeat after him, and Gabriel revealed to him the first verses of the Quran, those at the beginning of the Surah Al-Alaq: **"Proclaim! (or read!) in the name of thy Lord and Cherisher, Who created, Created man out of a (mere) clot of congealed blood. Proclaim! And thy Lord is Most Bountiful, He Who taught (the use of) the pen, Taught man that which he knew not."** (Surah 96:1-5)

Moreover, the Quran can only truly be understood if one uses the Hadiths and the commentary which clarifies when, where, and under what circumstances those particular passages were revealed. Therefore, if one merely read the translation of the Quran, the reader would not acquire the full meaning of the passages. Additionally, the reader would not know why a particular Surah or passage was revealed, or whether it has been omitted or abrogated. For example, those passages that ask the Muslims to kill all infidels or nonbelievers were revealed during wartime for specific battles and historical events. Hence, Muslims did not implement such verses after the particular passing of the battle or event. We know this to be true because within the Muslim world – a collection of nearly 60 countries – we find Christians, Jews, Buddhists, and atheists living amongst Muslims.

Another, and more appropriate example given the topic of fasting, is that there were two separate times in which fasting was commanded by God, both passages appearing in the same Surah. The first verse that asks Muslims to fast is found in Surah 2 verses 183-184. It states: **"O believers, fasting is prescribed for you, as it was prescribed for those before you, that you may be conscientious. And a ransom is incumbent upon those who are able, the feeding of a pauper. But if anyone willingly does even better, then that is better for him; yet it is better for you to fast, if you only knew."** If an individual chooses not to fast, they in turn must replace the fast by feeding the poor. This provision was rescinded and cancelled by verse 185, which was revealed a year later. This verse states, **"The month of Ramadan is the one in which the Quran was revealed, as guidance for humility, and demonstrations in the way of guidance and discrimination. So whoever among you is present that month should fast. If anyone is ill or on a journey, then the prescribed term is to be from other days. God wishes ease for you, not hardship; and that you fulfill the prescribed terms, and that you celebrate God for guiding you; and that you may be grateful."** Hence all Muslims are required, without due exception, to fast during Ramadan.

Chapter 3: Pillars of Islam

As stated in verse 183, fasting was required by earlier traditions. We know within the Abrahamic traditions, both Jews and Christians were mandated to fast. The fasts of Muslims and Jews are distinctly different from the fasts of Christians. For example, the Christian fasting is loosely interpreted to allow for some eating and drinking throughout the day – an individual can fast from a specific indulgence to meet the criterion for fasting. Moreover, Protestants do not have one standard for days, times or methods of fasting. While, on the other hand, Christians of the Catholic and Orthodox churches have the doctrine of fasting during Lent. Although Muslims are required to fast during the month of Ramadan, the Jews fast during specific holy days. Both Muslims and Jews fast approximately one hour before sunrise to sunset without any consumption of liquids or solids; such was the practice of the prophets. Prophet Moses fasted for forty days according to Deuteronomy 9:9, "When I went up to the mountain to receive the tablets of stone, the tablets of the covenant which the Lord had made with you, then I remained on the mountain forty days and nights; I neither ate bread nor drank water." Jesus Christ fasted for forty days and forty nights – which is demonstrated by Matthew 4:2, "And after He had fasted forty days and forty nights, He then became hungry." In both cases, neither Prophet Moses nor Prophet Jesus ate or drank anything. This is the fast that is followed by the Muslims just as it was taught by the Prophet Muhammad.

The intended goal of fasting is spiritual uplifting, so that one can bring themselves closer to God. Abstaining from food and physical intimacy is but a small part of fasting. Those are just the basic principles of the fast. The larger principle is the total awareness and submission to God. This will enable the spirit to be cleansed from the sins that have accumulated in the past year and replace them with the good that one is expected to do. Within this holy month, Muslims should increase their good works. Muslims are taught to be mindful of the unfortunate members of society. This includes the poor, the widowed, the sick, as well as orphans. During Ramadan, Muslims are asked to increase their gifts to these groups. In other words, be a good citizen, spread peace and joy amongst the people and do not neglect your obligations to the larger community. We are individuals within a larger context, whether as a nuclear family, extended family, or neighborhood. We are responsible for the well-being of the greater human population. At the same time, the fast is also an opportunity for humbling ourselves before God and submitting to Him by suppressing natural desires in order to please God. It is through His pleasure that one can hope to obtain a deeper spiritual relationship with God, leading to ultimate contentedness. Becoming closer to God with faith and good deeds is a result that fasting produces, and it is intended to recharge the spirit, to strive for goodness, and achieve spirituality. After the last fast is completed, Muslims celebrate the end of Ramadan with a celebration called Eid ul-Fitr, which is a large congregational prayer.

PILLAR FOUR: ZAKAT (TITHING)

"'Do not worship anything but God; and be good to parents, relatives, orphans, and the poor; and speak nicely to people, and pray regularly, and give alms.'" (Surah 2:83)

Zakat (charity) is the Islamic equivalent of the Christian and Jewish notion of tithing and is the third pillar of the Islamic faith. It literally comes from the root word *tazkiya* which means to purify or cleanse. An additional meaning of *tazkiya* is to multiply. As such, Zakat is the act of giving in charity that leads to the purification of our money, and this altruism of giving to others does not contribute to its diminution but to its increase. Islam comes from the perspective that all of our possessions (our wealth, our families, and even our bodies) are a trust from God that must be deployed in such a way that pleases Him. This principle of self-sacrifice to attain God's pleasure is a central theme that resonates throughout the Quran. By giving in charity to the needy, we as humans remain grounded to our true purpose of service to others. The act of hoarding and accumulation leads to selfishness, and this inclines the individual to think that his wealth is his birthright and will be with him forever. The kindly act of giving balances the individual and protects him/her from selfishness and greed. The recipient is aided by the gesture and good will is fostered between the parties. Zakat is also an opportunity to express gratitude to God for the bounty and comfort that He has bestowed.

Zakat is paid yearly and is required of all Muslims on their savings. As such, the payment of Zakat is not obligatory on one's property but on the excess savings which are calculated by deducting all debts and expenses. It is 2.5% or 1/40th of one's savings. The Quran specifies in the clearest of terms to whom this charity can be given. The Quran states:

"Zakat is for the poor and the needy, and those employed to manage the funds, for those whose hearts are reconciled to the truth, for manumitting a slave, and for the freedom of captives, and those in debt, and for fighters in the cause of God, and for the wayfarer. It is so ordered by God, and God is

All-Knowing, All Wise." (Surah 9:60)

The verse stipulates the various categories of the poor and the manner in which Zakat is to be used. It cannot be given to an institution, and unlike giving tithing to churches, Zakat cannot be given to mosques or Islamic centers. It can only be given to the poor and the needy of a community. The wisdom behind this is that institutions use a portion of their money for the upkeep and management of their organization. Phrased plainly, they have certain fixed costs and fixed expenses. A mosque, for instance, has to pay for its light bill, heating and water expenses, etc. and such expenditure of money does not alleviate the plight of the poor and destitute. In order to directly assist the disenfranchised members of a community, Zakat can only be given to the categories mentioned above. Voluntary charity (or *sadaqa*) can be given to mosques, churches, humanitarian relief organizations, and so forth.

This term *sadaqa* which is loosely translated as "voluntary charity" has a holistic meaning in Islam. It refers to any charitable act that helps others in some way. In a famous quote narrated by Abu Dharr below, the Prophet Muhammad captured this comprehensive understanding of charity:

> "Some of the companions of the Messenger of God said: O Messenger of God, the affluent have made off with the rewards. They pray as we pray, they fast as we fast, and they give away in charity the superfluity of their wealth.
>
> He said: Has not God made things for you to give away in charity? Truly every act of glorifying God is a charity, to recognize and proclaim that God is the greatest is a charity, every utterance praising God is a charity, and the testimony that there is only One God is a charity. To enjoin good action is a charity, to forbid an evil action is a charity, and in the sexual act of each of you there is a charity.
>
> They said: O Messenger of God, when one of us fulfills his sexual desire, will he have some reward for that? He said: Do you not think that were he to act upon it unlawfully he would be sinning? Likewise, if he has acted upon it lawfully, he will have a reward." (Muslim)

In this text, it is clear that charity has been conceptualized in a comprehensive manner. Since no man is an island, he/she has to constantly interact with other beings. Thus charity is not narrowly defined in terms of giving money to people. Instead, every act of enjoining good, every act of prohibiting evil, and every kind gesture is considered to be charity, Such acts enable us to fulfill our obligations to others and contribute to the enrichment of social relationships. This is analogous to the prophetic teaching of Jesus Christ when he said, "What you do to the least of my brothers you do to me." Here, any harm inflicted on the weakest and disenfranchised members of a community is considered to be an attack on Jesus himself. Likewise, any act of good will toward others is divinely sanctified and fulfills our moral imperative as human beings.

Money is not the only means by which one can tithe. Words and deeds are also instrumental. As with anything, Islam enjoins moderation. Concerning giving alms, the Quran prescribes the servant to be fair and not gravitate to extremes. The Quran states, "And do not make your hand tied to your neck (like a miser), nor extend it to its utmost so that you become worthy of blame and penniless." This verse teaches that we should not be so stingy such that our hands are tied behind our necks. At the same time, we should not extend our hands outward in such a way that relinquishes all of our possessions. Between the two extremes of extravagance and miserliness is a moderate path that helps the recipient and yet protects the rights of the giver. Of course, the ultimate goal is to create a social order on earth that is rooted in justice and does not lead to the hoarding of wealth by a few. In this regard, the Quran states "What God has granted (as booty) to His Messenger belongs to God, to His Messenger, and to relatives and the orphans, the needy and the wayfarer in order that it may not be circulated between the wealthy among you."

It is estimated that there are over a billion people on earth who are overweight. Simultaneously there are over 800,000,000 people worldwide who are starving and living in extreme poverty. How can these two contradictions coexist? The reality is that there isn't a shortage of food and resources in the world, but rather, a lack of kindness and empathy toward others. Humans need to internalize the sentiment of social empathy, and this is what Zakat seeks to cultivate.

One final thought with regards to tithing is that individuals must not be persuaded by preachers who obtain enormous amounts of wealth from their parishioners. Any tithing is intended for the poor and indigent of society—not to support the extravagant lifestyles of preachers. It is troubling to see well-intended and kind parishioners give their hard-earned money to televangelists, who then become rich. A great example of abusive fundraising conducted by televangelists is Oral Roberts, who blackmailed supporters to give in excess of 8 million dollars over several months. Roberts claimed that if this goal was not met, God would "call him up" (Posner 49). This is an extremely offensive use of religion, God, and the church. Indeed, this accusation can be extended to many other church leaders, such as Rod Parsley, Pat Robertson, and John Hagee.

A quintessential example of the opulence displayed by these preachers is Rod Parsley, who lives in a 7,500 sq. ft. home that is worth over one million dollars and flies in a private jet that was provided at his church's expense (Posner, 2). Also, John Hagee received 800,000 dollars in compensation for his services from his non-profit organization and his church in 2004 (Posner, 4). Islam holds these people accountable for their lifestyles and giving to them would be considered sinful, as it contributes to their sinful accumulation of wealth, opulent lifestyles, and their profitable marketing of religion.

PILLAR FIVE: HAJJ (PILGRIMAGE TO MECCA)

"In it are Signs Manifest; (for example), the Station of Abraham; whoever enters it attains security; Pilgrimage thereto is a duty men owe to God,- those who can afford the journey; but if any deny faith, God stands not in need of any of His creatures." (Surah 3:97)

The fifth and final Pillar of Islam is the Hajj or pilgrimage to Mecca. Muslims are required to perform the Hajj at least once in their lifetimes if they are capable physically and financially of doing so. Hence, every year 2.5 – 3 million Muslims congregate to Mecca on the twelfth month of each year called Dhul-Hijjah. The pilgrimage predates Prophet Muhammad going far back to the time of Prophets Abraham and Ishmael. If you recall the biblical narrative discussed in chapter one, Sarah after the birth of Isaac told Abraham to drive out this maid Hagar and her son Ishmael. At which point, Abraham took both Hagar and Ishmael to the land of the east. However, the Muslims believe that this is a negative portrayal of both Hagar and Ishmael, suggesting that they are not good company for Isaac. Muslims believe, when Ishmael was a child, God commanded Abraham to take Hagar into what is now Mecca. In Genesis 21:19, it is stated that when Hagar "opened her eyes...she saw a well of water; and she went and filled the skin with water and gave the lad a drink." These two people became the first inhabitants of a desolate land surrounded by hills. It was through Hagar and through Ishmael that nomadic people began to settle around this new source of water in the vast desert. These people later became the Arabs.

    The pilgrimage to Mecca is significant because it became the holy city when Abraham and Ishmael built the Kabba. Since both Abraham and Ishmael entered into the covenant of worshipping the one God, they constructed the first house of worship called the Kabba. The word Kabba means cube, and it is a small black structure. Muslim scholars believe that the Kabba was rebuilt on the foundation that had been set by Adam, but was buried during Noah's flood. It was Abraham and Ishmael that reconstructed it upon its original foundation. However, as documented in the Quran as well as the Bible, since the Kabba was built it has been a holy place of worship and a sight of pilgrimage. There is a reference in the Psalms of David that refers to the pilgrimage to Mecca. In Psalm 84:5-6, David states, "How blessed is the man whose strength is in you, in whose heart are the highways to Zion! Passing through the valley of Bakka they make it a spring." The word Bakka is another name given to Mecca depending on the dialect. The Quran also refers to Mecca as Bakka in Surah 3:96. The verse states, **"The first House (of worship) appointed for men was that at Bakka."** There are rich written and oral traditions that give importance to the Kabba and make the city of Mecca holy. Hence, Muslims must make a pilgrimage to Mecca and reenact those traditions passed on from Abraham through subsequent generations and continued by Prophet Muhammad. Thus, for more than 1400 years Muslims from all over the world gather during the twelfth month, Dhul-Hijjah, and act out the various traditions and rituals—which usually take approximately ten days. When the individual puts on the traditional two piece white garment known as *ihram*, the pilgrimage starts. There is no traditional garment requirement for women. The *ihram* has to be two unstitched pieces of clothing; it is worn during Hajj to signify the equality of all peoples in that no one wearing an *ihram* can determine whether any one is a king, servant, or of the lower or upper classes. This traditional garment is believed to be worn by Abraham, and as such, Muslims have adopted it for the pilgrimage. The *ihram* also symbolizes the burial garment worn at the time of death. It is a reminder to the pilgrims of the certainty of death, inevitability of resurrection, and accountability before God. Hence, the realization that our lives on Earth are ephemeral and the true existence is the hereafter becomes crystallized. There is a realization that Muslim people are one people sharing one experience and no one is greater or superior to any other. Therefore, there is a strong emphasis on seeking forgiveness for one's sins, and humbling oneself before God. As the *ihram* is worn, anger, fighting, or taking of any life is prohibited, even if the life belongs to an animal or plant. Life is sacred in and around the Kabba at all times, and this is especially the case during the month of Hajj. The Hajj is a series of rituals and traditions that signify a particular event. I will discuss two such events that are part of the Abrahamic and Ishmaelite traditions.

As mentioned earlier, Abraham relocated Hagar and son Ishmael. He then constructed the Kabba and encircled it seven times. Thus, every pilgrim during the Hajj must circle the Kabba seven times in Abraham's memory. It is only done, to my knowledge, out of respect to Abraham and the Kabba. Another important tradition is the sacrifice of a sheep or ram, which occurs at the end of the Hajj. This sacrifice is in remembrance of Abraham's story in which God instructed him to sacrifice his son. In both the Christian and Muslim narratives, God replaced his son with a sheep. However, Christians and Jews believe that the son that Abraham was supposed to sacrifice was Isaac. This is supported in Genesis 22:2, "He said, 'Take now your son, your only son, whom you love, Isaac, and go to the land of Moriah, and offer him there as a burnt offering on one of the mountains of which I will tell you.'" If you examine this verse closely, it says your only son Isaac. However, Isaac was not his only son. Abraham had Ishmael 14 years before Isaac's birth. Both Christians and Jews argue that Isaac was the son born to Sarah, Abraham's wife, and as such is Abraham's only son. However, that does not mean that Abraham had only one son. Moreover, there is nowhere in the Bible that says Ishmael and Medean were not Abraham's sons. To say that Ishmael and Medean were lesser sons of Abraham because they were not born to Sarah is an obvious inconsistency. The truth, Muslims believe, is that it was Ishmael who was supposed to be sacrificed by Abraham. Neither the Jews nor the Christians remember or honor this sacrifice of Abraham. Even before Islam, the Arabs had honored and respected this sacrifice of Ishmael, and during the pilgrimage, Muslims sacrificed an animal in the memory of that historical event. Of course, Prophet Muhammad, being a prophet and a descendent of Abraham and Ishmael, kept this sacrifice and tradition. The Quran and Hadiths, the sayings of Prophet Muhammad are rich with details regarding this particular historical event. In Surah 37 verses 102-109 we read:

> **"Then when he had come of age to work together, he said, 'My son, I see in a dream that I sacrifice you. Now let's see what you think.' He said, 'Father, do what you are commanded; you will find me, God willing, bearing it calmly.' Then when both had acquiesced and he lay him**

> down, on his forehead, We called to him, 'Abraham! You have already authenticated the vision.' For that is how We recompense those who do right; for this was certainly an evident trial, as We redeemed him through a tremendous sacrifice, and We left for him in future generations 'Peace upon Abraham!'"

Through this verse we learn that Abraham had a dream in which he was sacrificing Ishmael as a test from God of his faith and obedience. Before we get to the response of Ishmael, some may think it is rather absurd for one to sacrifice his or her son based on a dream. However, Muslims believe that dreams are also a source of revelation to Prophets. In the case of any prophet, their greater cause is the service and obedience to God. All prophets go through tests and tribulations, and each and every prophet has increased their faith and status as a result of it. No prophet of God has, as a result of such tests, disobeyed God, and became unfaithful. Of course, some tests are greater than others. In the case of Abraham, he had one of the greatest tests from God, in which he had to sacrifice Ishmael. Moreover, one should not overlook the magnitude of the faith and obedience of Ishmael when he said, "**Father, do what you are commanded; you will find me, God willing, bearing it calmly.**" This verse demonstrates the great love and devotion that he had for his father and the tremendous faith and obedience that Ishmael had towards Almighty God. It is for this reason that both Abraham and Ishmael are paradigms of faith and obedience.

One final point regarding Abraham and Ishmael relates to the prayer that they made while building the Kabba. In Surah 2:126, we read **"And Abraham said, 'My Lord, make this a secure city; and feed its people with fruits, whoever of them believe in God and the last day.'"** It is interesting that as Abraham and Ishmael were building the Kabba – the Quran records one of Abraham's prayers. What is remarkable about this verse is that Mecca and where the Kabba was built was a complete desert wilderness. There was no life for hundreds of miles. It is quite remarkable how fast that area became the center of commerce in the Arab peninsula, and a place where people also congregated. In fact, the word Mecca is now synonymous with 'the center.' Moreover, Abraham's prayer included that Mecca would become a place of abundance in order to sustain a prosperous community whose inhabitants would be able to worship in peace and live off the land. This too seems to have been realized, as the region is rich with oil, gold, and other valuable minerals. In closing, there are many more rituals and traditions of Abraham that have been passed down that are a part of the Hajj that

Chapter 3: Pillars of Islam

Muslims perform. There are numerous books that discuss the rituals of the Hajj extensively. The purpose of this chapter was to examine how the five pillars of Islam correspond with the Abrahamic traditions.

Part two will carefully analyze the Quranic passages concerning Jesus Christ.

Christ Jesus, The Son of Mary: A Muslim Perspective

Part 2

Prophet Jesus in the Quran

4

Al-Baqara

(The Cow)

In part two of this book, we will examine Quranic passages to explain the Muslim position regarding Prophet Jesus. Again, Islam is the only major non-Christian religion that makes it an article of faith to believe in Jesus Christ. His birth, teachings, miracles, and life story are preserved in the Quran. In sharing these accounts, I hope to demonstrate his reverential status in Islam. Moreover, after reading the pages that follow, we will be familiar with a different perspective and learn the additional details on Jesus and his family contained in the Quran. I also hope that you will realize that the Muslim perspective is consistent and well substantiated. Conversely, Christianity since its formation and until today has had numerous contradictory beliefs and practices among its followers. A powerful testimony that affirms this fact is the thousands of denominations and churches that exist throughout the Christian world. However, Muslims are unified in their beliefs concerning Prophet Jesus, without exception. The reason for this remarkable unanimity and consistency is due to the clarity of the Quran and Prophet Muhammad's teachings. Thus, we will first look to the Quran and analyze each verse that refers to Prophet Jesus.

There are very few accurate and reliable English translations of the Quran, and I only recommend the following: Yusuf Ali, Muhammad Asad, Thomas Cleary, M. A. S. Abdel Haleem, Ahmed Zaki Hammad, Syed Vickar Ahamed, and Marmaduke Pickthall. This book uses the Thomas Cleary because it is the most approachable translation. Other than the verses on Jesus, we will also analyze the verses pertaining to Mary, Prophet Zachariah, and his son Prophet Yahya (John the Baptist) as they are a central part in the life of Prophet Jesus.

Chapter 4: Al-Baqara (The Cow)

By now one should realize the Quran was revealed to Prophet Muhammad through the Angel Gabriel over a 23 year period. You may also remember that the Quran does not follow a chronological sequence but it is laid out as instructed by Angel Gabriel to Prophet Muhammad. As such, I think it would be appropriate to begin with the first reference to Prophet Jesus found in Surah 2 verse 87 and work our way up to the last mention of Prophet Jesus' name appearing in Surah 61 verse 14. Let us begin with this first verse and follow accordingly.

Before we discuss the verses in chapter 2, some background details are first necessary. Surah 2 is the longest chapter in the Quran and it was revealed in the first two years of Prophet Muhammad's migration to the city of Medina (624-625). The Surah is called Al-Baqara or "The Cow" because in verse 67 the word cow is mentioned in which Prophet Moses instructed the Sons of Jacob to sacrifice a cow. To a Western reader unfamiliar with the Quran, the chapter titles may seem awkward and unusual. The reality is that the titles of the various Surahs are derived from the mention of a particular reference or event discussed within the respective Surah. For purposes of clarification, each verse stands out by itself and the subheading is italicized. With this in mind, the first verse again is Surah 2 verse 87.

> **"We gave Moses the Book, and We had messengers follow up after him. And We gave Jesus Son of Mary clear proofs and strengthened him with the Holy Spirit. Is it that whenever a messenger comes to you with what your selves do not like, you are scornful? Some of them you called liars, some of them you killed."**

There are a few important points that need to be highlighted. First, to fully understand this verse we need to know the preceding passages. Beginning with verse 40, God enumerates historical accounts of the disobedience of the Sons of Jacob. One reason this is done is to teach Muslims how not to behave disobediently and to reinforce the faith of the newly converted Muslims in Medina. To reaffirm that Prophet Muhammad is the true messenger of God, the Quran provides numerous details of earlier prophets, and in particular, prophetic stories of the Sons of Jacob. This is done to remove falsehoods attributed to the prophets that are found in the Old Testament. For instance, some of the falsehoods include: portraying Prophet Abraham worshipping idols, Noah and Lot having relations with their daughters, and David and Solomon having adulterous affairs.

Since the Quran is the completion of divine revelation, the Quran corrects the distortions of previous scriptures and restores the elevated position of prophets.

God is also warning Jewish communities of Medina to acknowledge the prophet hood of Prophet Muhammad and not to repeat the mistakes of their forefathers who sinned against God. However, the Quran admonishes that if they were to continue in their rebellion, then God would punish them. Verse 86 states, **"They are the ones who take the life of this world in exchange for the Hereafter; so their torment will not be eased, and they will not be delivered."** The case for their punishment is laid out in verse 87. Despite possessing divine revelation given to them by Prophet Moses and other prophets that were sent to them, they nevertheless puffed up with pride and denied some prophets while killing others.

The singling out of Prophet Jesus is significant because God chooses him as one of the most important prophets sent to the Sons of Jacob. They had been anticipating the coming of the Messiah for over 1,000 years. The treatment of Prophet Jesus best illustrates the actions of the Jews toward God's messengers. God emphasizes that He gave Prophet Jesus clear signs so that they may have faith. But despite seeing the miracles that he performed, the Jews puffed up with pride, denied that he was the Messiah, and ultimately "crucified" him.

Additionally, I would like to draw attention to God calling Prophet Jesus "the son of Mary." The significance of this is to deny the Christian belief that he is the "son of God." Virtually every time that the name Jesus appears in the Quran, it is followed up by "son of Mary." Also, no other prophet has been linked to a parent the way Jesus is in the Quran. Phrased simply, the Quran does not state, for example: Isaac the son of Abraham, Solomon the son of David, Ishmael the son of Abraham and Yahya the son of Zachariah. However, there are two exceptions in which the linkage to a parent was necessary. In both cases, the reference is to a group of people. The Quran uses the sons (children) of Adam and the sons of Jacob to refer to a category of people, and not an individual. However, Prophet Jesus is mentioned with his mother (i.e., Jesus, the son of Mary). The exception to this is when his name follows in a sequence of other prophets, as in the verse below.

"And Zachariah and John, and Jesus and Elias. Each of them had integrity." (Surah 6:85)

A similar passage appears in Surah 42 entitled "The Consultation."

> "God has prescribed for you what God enjoined on Noah, by which We inspired you, and what We enjoined on Abraham, Moses, and Jesus, that you be steadfast in faith and not be disunited in it. What you call them to is too much for idolaters. God chooses for God whomever God wants, and guides to the divine whoever turns to God." (Surah 42:13)

The final point regarding verse 87 that needs mentioning is the reference to the Holy Spirit. The Holy Spirit in the Quran refers to Angel Gabriel who gave strength to Prophet Jesus. Gabriel literally means the "strength of God" in Hebrew. In Islam, he is the highest ranking angel since he is responsible for the conveyance of revelation. In the Bible, however, the Holy Spirit indeed also performs the same function as the inspirer of revelation but is not considered to be Angel Gabriel. In addition, the strength given to Prophet Jesus through Angel Gabriel was used to perform miracles of clear signs of God's sovereignty. The role that Angel Gabriel played in the life of Prophet Jesus will be examined in subsequent verses.

> "They say, 'Become Jews or Christians, and you will be guided.' Say, 'But the religion of Abraham is rightly oriented; he was not an idolater.' Say, 'We believe in God, and what was revealed to us, and what was revealed to Abraham, Ishmael, Isaac, Jacob, and the Tribes, and what was given to Moses and Jesus, and what was given to the prophets from their Lord. We do not make a distinction between any of them; we acquiesce to God.'" (Surah 2:135-136)

As previously mentioned, it is important to know the context and circumstances of a particular passage in order to fully comprehend the meaning. With this in mind, a few thoughts arise concerning the above verses. The passages that precede 135 and 136 were addressing a critical issue that existed in Arabia. It seems that the idol worshipping Arabs, the Jews, and the Christians all claimed to be following the religion and traditions of Prophet Abraham. The Arabs claimed that they were the true followers of Prophet Abraham because they venerated the Kabba, which again was the sacred structure built by Abraham and Ishmael. Also, the Arabs provided food and shelter to those who visited the Kabba during the pilgrimage. Concurrently, the Jews and Christians believed that they were the true followers of Prophet Abraham because they were the direct descendants and possessors of the sacred scriptures. Thus, to provide clarity to this issue, God responds to the Jews and Christians who say **"Become Jews or Christians, and you will be guided."** God then orders the Muslims to respond in the following manner: **"But the religion of Abraham is rightly oriented; he was not an idolater."**

This retort conveys without equivocation that Prophet Abraham was never engaged in idol worship as portrayed in the Old Testament. In fact, the Quran teaches that Prophet Abraham left his homeland Ur because he was a vociferous opponent of their idolatry. However, both Jews and Christians have exhibited in their past the tendency to worship idols. Pertaining to the Jews, we read in Kings 17:12 "They served idols, concerning which the Lord had said to them, 'You shall not do this thing.'" Christians would also be accused of worshiping multiple gods because they associate Jesus Christ and the Holy Spirit with God. However, Prophet Abraham never worshipped other Gods except the One true unseen God. Therefore, in verse 135, Muslims are reclaiming the religion of Prophet Abraham by worshipping the One transcendental God as he did. In verse 136, God pronounces the Muslim creed.

Regarding verse 136, three important points need to be enunciated. First, Muslims believe in the One and only Almighty God and the revelation sent to the people through His messengers. Since Prophet Muhammad had the Quran revealed to him; we naturally accept his message first. By the same token, we as Muslims must also believe in the revelations given to the other prophets as they too were sent from God. God is the single source of the revelations given to all prophets. Since we believe in the previous scriptures, one may ask, "Why, then, don't you follow them"? This is a good segue to the second point.

The fact that Muslims believe in the revelations given to Prophets Abraham, Ishmael, Isaac, Jacob, Moses, David, Jesus and others does not mean that we must obey their laws. This is because when God sends revelation through His prophets it applies only to that particular community. Otherwise, God would have sent only one book for all to follow. In 2 Chronicles 36:15 it states "The Lord, the God of their fathers, sent word to them again and again by His messengers, because He had compassion on His people and on His dwelling place." Muslim scholars believe that God sent about 100 *Suhuf* or scrolls and four major books. The four Holy Books are: the Torah – first five books of the Old Testament given to Prophet Moses, the Zaboor given to Prophet David, the Ingeel or Gospel given to Prophet Jesus, and the Quran given to Prophet Muhammad who was given the final revelation from God. As far as the *Suhuf* (scrolls) are concerned, we have no names or whereabouts of their existence. Nevertheless, Muslims are required to believe in them. However, the most famous *Suhuf* mentioned in the Quran is that of Prophet Abraham. It would not surprise me if most Jews and Christians do not even know that Prophet Abraham also received divine revelation that he and his people were expected to follow. To such people, let me refer them to the Old Testament. Genesis 26:4-5 "... and by your descendants all the nations of the earth shall be blessed; because Abraham obeyed Me and kept My charge, My commandments, My statues and My laws." These laws, statutes, and commandments that Prophet Abraham obeyed were given to him and his people and they were obeyed until God sent another prophet either adding to them or completely replacing them. This is in direct contradiction to the Christian belief that there was no divine revelation or law from Adam to Moses, as stated in Romans 5:13-14, "For until the Law sin was in the world, but sin is not imputed when there is no law. Nevertheless death reigned from Adam until Moses, even over those who had not sinned." Muslims reject this Paulian construct, as we believe that prophets came to guide the people to the path of God. In doing so, instruction on matters of faith and worship and the moral teachings were passed. That being said, after Prophet Abraham, we know that Isaac and Jacob received revelation for their faithful community to follow. This was the case until Prophet Moses was given the Torah to be obeyed by the Children of Israel. This new law abrogated the old. The reason for the replacement of God's commandments was that the *Suhufs* were intended for a small group for a particular time period. Hence, as the Abrahamic community grew into a large society, the Sons of Jacob then received a new set of laws to fit their circumstances and times. However, the Torah contained onerous restrictions that God had placed on the Sons of Jacob. Because of it, God gave Prophet David the Zaboor and the Ingeel to Prophet Jesus which eased some of the austere restrictions. Therefore, the statement of Prophet Jesus in Matthew 5:17 makes sense from this viewpoint. Here Jesus said, "Do not think that I came to abolish the Law or the Prophets; I did not come to abolish but to fulfill." Observe that the above mentioned books were given exclusively to the Jewish people. But what about the Gentiles? God in His infinite justice sent Prophet Muhammad as the final messenger of God. He was given the final revelation, the Quran, which is to be followed by all people and it is the primary authority for Muslims. In essence, we believe in the revelation given to all the prophets but Muslims are only required to follow and obey the Quran.

The final point on verse 136 pertains to the last sentence, **"We do not make a distinction between any of them."** Muslims are required not only to believe in the sacred books given to earlier prophets but we accept all of them as messengers of God. Muslims do not pick and choose the prophets for acceptance and denial. On the other hand, Jews as well as Christians are guilty of this prejudice. The Jews, for example, denied Prophet Jesus as a prophet and the Messiah. Likewise, the Christians deny Prophet Muhammad as the final messenger of God. However, Muslims acknowledge, respect, and believe in all of the prophets and messengers of God and the revelations given to them. We believe this because we acquiesce to God as stated in verse 136.

> **"Those are signs of God, which We recite to you in truth. And you are indeed one of the messengers. Some of those messengers We favored over others; God spoke to one of them, and elevated others to ranks of honor. And We gave the proofs to Jesus, son of Mary, and We fortified him with the Holy Spirit. And if God had willed, those who came after them would not have fought after the proofs came to them; but they disagreed, and some of them believed while some of them scoffed. And if God had wished, they would not have fought; but God acts on divine will."** (Surah 2:252-253)

To put these passages in proper perspective, the verses that proceeded 252 and 253 dealt with the accounts of the battle that took place between Sol and the faithful Jews numbering approximately 313 versus Goliath and his army of more than 100,000. The details of this battle are similar to what is mentioned in the Bible when young David kills the army general Goliath causing his army to flee making Sol and the Jews victorious and David emerging as a hero. However, the rancor that is portrayed in the biblical account between Sol and David does not exist in the Muslim tradition. Muslims would categorically deny animosity between two men of God. Sol was a king chosen by God and David a prophet. As such, they would be righteous and God-fearing and not vindictive and unscrupulous. The Quran shares this historical event to teach the nascent Muslim community that if the Muslims were faithful and obedient, God would also give them victory, as He did with Sol's army.

Chapter 4: Al-Baqara (The Cow)

Also, as mentioned previously, sharing these detailed accounts of past events validates Prophet Muhammad as the true messenger of God. The fact that Prophet Muhammad reveals so much information with great specificity is in itself a testimony to his prophet hood. Keep in mind that the Arabs did not have the concept of prophets like the Jews and Christians and nor did they have any revelation from God that told them about the earlier prophets. After all, they had not received any divine guidance since Ishmael over 2,500 years prior. Prophet Muhammad was unlettered and did not know how to read and write. Yet he gave the Arabs this knowledge with truth and accuracy. The word truth is used in verse 252 to illustrate that the Quran is not filled with lies and inaccuracies of prophets. Unlike the Quran, the Bible contains extensive family genealogies as well as sexual narrations which are blasphemous and abhorrent. Hence, in verse 252 God states, **"Those are signs of God, which We recite to you in truth. And you are indeed one of the messengers."** With this verse God confirms that Prophet Muhammad receives divine revelation and he is a prophet among a number of prophets.

In verse 253 we learn that in the eyes of God there is a rank and hierarchy among His messengers. God in particular identifies two prophets who are dear to Him because of the special gifts that were bestowed upon them. The rank and nearness to God was not necessarily due to anything that they had done per se. Rather, it was God from His bounty who gave them a status that made them special through the gifts that he provided. God stated in verse 253, **"Some of those messengers We favored over others; God spoke to one of them, and elevated others to ranks of honor. And We gave the proofs to Jesus, son of Mary, and We fortified him with the Holy Spirit."** Clearly, Prophet Moses achieved an elevated station by virtue of God speaking directly to him. This is a gift that had not been given to any other prophet on earth until Prophet Moses. I specify here, "on earth," because we know that Prophet Adam communicated with God in heaven. Moreover, Muslims believe that Prophet Muhammad also communicated with God directly when he was lifted up into the heavens. This event called Mairaj (also known as the Night Journey) took place in Mecca shortly before the Prophet's migration to Medina. Muslims believe Angel Gabriel took the Prophet first to Medina to show him his new home. Afterwards, Prophet Muhammad was taken to Jerusalem where he led the congregational prayer of all the prophets. After the prayer, Prophet Muhammad ascended into the heavens with Angel Gabriel and God spoke to the Prophet directly. Perhaps this may seem out of the ordinary to some, but the Bible has Elijah and Enoch both being lifted up into heaven. The same is true of Prophet Jesus when Angel Gabriel lifted him to the heavens. However, Prophet Moses communicated not in the heavens but on earth. Every other prophet communicated with God through the Angel Gabriel. It was the exclusive responsibility of Angel Gabriel to be the conduit of the divine messages. And even in the Bible it was Angel Gabriel who brought divine revelation to prophets. In Luke 1:19 it states, "The angel answered and said to him, "I am Gabriel, who stands in the presence of God, and I have been sent to speak to you and to bring you this good news."

Therefore, this blessing of divine communication that was given to Prophet Moses makes him more special and gives him a status above other prophets. Verse 253 also singled out Prophet Jesus as having a higher status among the prophets for having been given clear signs and being strengthened with the Holy Spirit (Angel Gabriel). The significance of Prophet Jesus among many emanates from the numerous and multifarious miracles that he performed. These miracles that are discussed in the Quran were done in order to demonstrate to the Jewish people that he was the true Messiah and prophet of God. Thus, God's abundant blessings given to Prophet Jesus bestow him a high status among prophets. The Quran says that God strengthened him with the Holy Spirit. God assigned Angel Gabriel to him for the performance of miracles and for his protection from the Jews who were conspiring to murder yet another prophet.

Both Prophet Moses and Jesus are examples in the Quran to illustrate that in God's eyes there is a rank among the prophets and not all are equal, as Verse 253 clearly asserts. However, one should not take from this verse that only Prophets Moses and Jesus have a high status alone. Muslim theologians believe that there were over 125,000 messengers of God sent to the various tribes, nations, and peoples from Adam to Prophet Muhammad. But the Quran names only 25 of them. Along with Prophets Moses and Jesus, Muslims believe that Prophet Muhammad, Abraham, and Noah also have a celebrated status with God because of the blessings given to them. However, Muslims are instructed not to discuss the various ranks of prophets because this falls under the purview of God's knowledge alone. Furthermore, any attempt to extrapolate the status of God's prophets will inevitably disrespect another prophet. Thus, we love, revere, and believe in all of the prophets that the Quran names as well as those prophets that the Quran does not mention. Regarding Prophet Muhammad's rank, he was the final prophet of God and he was sent for all of mankind. He and the Quran will be witnesses on the Day of Judgment to the truth of divine revelation and prophetic guidance. Also, Prophet Muhammad performed many miracles that are mentioned in the Quran and the Hadith collection. Finally, Prophet Muhammad

Chapter 4: Al-Baqara (The Cow)

is the *Sayyed* or "honorary leader" of all the prophets. To conclude, the universal Muslim position is that Prophet Muhammad has a very high rank with God.

5

Aal-E-Imran

(The Family of Imran)

Surah 3 is called the Family of Imran and was revealed in Medina. Imran was the father of Mary and the Surah chronicles her story. Although the Bible does not have any record of the name of her father, there is an association through an obscure gospel that identifies Joachim as being her father. Little is known about him or his wife Anna. The Quran, on the other hand, provides great details about Lady Mary's life. But before we address those verses, let us first examine verse 3 of Surah 3. The Surah begins with the exaltations of the Almighty God in the first two verses. Then in verse 3 God says, **"God revealed the Book to you in truth, verifying what was before it; God revealed the Torah and the Gospel before as guidance for humanity; and God revealed the Criterion."** There are three points I would like to make regarding verse 3.

First, although I have mentioned it before: the Quran was revealed to Prophet Muhammad over a period of 23 years. Unlike the 10 commandments which God gave to Prophet Moses all at once, the Quran was revealed in a piecemeal manner as circumstances arose. Second, the Quran confirms those divine revelations that preceded it, mainly the Torah and the Ingeel (the Gospel). It does this on two levels. On a very basic level the Quran affirms that God had sent down divine revelation in the past to the prophets. In verse 3 God mentions the Torah and the Ingeel as being two examples of earlier scriptures. However, more profoundly, the Quran confirms the Torah and the Ingeel by acknowledging their essential teachings. In other words, the universal teachings among the three traditions are virtually identical. The followers of these three books share the following: belief in one God, angels, prophets, miracles, Day of Judgment, social morality, and so forth. Thus, the Quran is the truth from God confirming the core teachings of the previous books that had been sent down by Him. Because the source of these three Holy Scriptures is the One God, the core teachings naturally overlap and close parallels can be observed.

This is not to suggest that strident differences do not exist. In fact, there are questions regarding the authenticity of the current Torah and the Ingeel (the Gospel). For instance, the Muslim position regarding these books is that we acknowledge that they were Holy Books, but they were not properly preserved by the scribes. I do not wish to offend anyone, but the reality is that both books have been corrupted and lost at one point. The Torah had been lost for centuries and discovered by Jewish scholars who could not read it or understand it. As found in 2 Chronicles, "When they were bringing out the money which had been brought into the house of the Lord, Hilkiah the priest found the book of the law of the Lord given by Moses" (34:14). Concerning the Ingeel (the Gospel) given to Prophet Jesus, it must first be clearly understood that Christians do not believe that any scripture was produced by Prophet Jesus as divine revelation from God. What Christians do have are the Gospels according to Matthew, Mark, Luke and John. By contrast, Muslims believe that there was The Gospel given to Prophet Jesus called the Ingeel which he gave to his followers. Although Christians may be quick to dismiss it, there are nevertheless numerous verses that clearly indicate that Prophet Jesus was given divine revelation.

In John 15:15 it states, "But I have called you friends, for *all things that I have heard from My Father* I have made known to you." This would be the Ingeel and the Gospel of Prophet Jesus Christ. Again, Muslims believe that Prophets receive revelation from God through the Angel Gabriel and he delivers the divine word. The word of God that Prophet Muhammad heard though Angel Gabriel is called the Quran. Likewise, the word of God that Prophet Jesus heard and conveyed to the people is called the Ingeel or the Gospel. Moreover, John 12:49-50 makes mentions of God "the father" teaching Prophet Jesus what to say and speak. It states, "For I did not speak on my own initiative, but the Father Himself who sent me has given me a *commandment as what to say and what to speak*. I know that His commandment is eternal life; therefore the things I speak, I speak *just as the Father has told me*." We also read in John 8:26 and 28 which states, "I have many things to speak and to judge concerning you, but He who sent Me is true; and the *things which I heard from Him,* these I speak to the world ... So Jesus said, "When you lift up the Son of Man, then you will know that I am He, and I do nothing on My own initiative, but I speak these things as *The Father taught Me.*" In both John 8:26 and 28 and 12:49-50 it becomes very clear that God was speaking through Prophet Jesus and that which he spoke would be called divine revelation. Therefore, God's teaching conveyed to Prophet Jesus becomes the Ingeel, The Gospel of Prophet Jesus. Furthermore, the fact that Prophet Jesus is taught confirms that he is not God but one who is completely dependent upon Him for knowledge and guidance.

We learn from the above passages not only did Prophet Jesus receive revelation but that anything he did was not by his own initiative but by the command of the Almighty. Does this dependency on the part of Prophet Jesus Christ appear that he is God himself? The true reality is that Prophet Jesus was told what to say and speak which Muslims call divine revelation. Phrased plainly, anything that Prophet Jesus heard from God would be the divine word, or the Ingeel. As such, the Gospels of the New Testament are not the *actual* Ingeel given to Prophet Jesus. The Gospels of Matthew, Mark, Luke, and John are **versions** of the Gospel and are according to them. This is why the Bible has "The Gospel According to Matthew," "The Gospel According to Mark," and so forth. In fact, Luke conducted research before writing his version of the Gospel. In Luke 1:3, it states, "It seemed fitting for me as well, having investigated everything carefully from the beginning, to write it out for you in consecutive order…" Therefore, each of the Gospels indeed contains *part* of the Ingeel that the Quran confirms. Whatever happened to the original Gospel of Prophet Jesus?

In light of what has been presented thus far, the reader should consider two important verses from the Gospel according to Mark. As you think about them, ask yourself whether "the Gospel" being mentioned in these verses refer to the Gospels of Matthew, Mark, Luke, and John; or the Gospels' of Thomas or Barnabas? Mark 1:15 states, "And saying, 'The time is fulfilled, and the kingdom of God is at hand; repent and *believe in the gospel*.'" And Mark 8:35 says, "For whoever wishes to save his life will lose it, but whoever loses his life for my sake and the gospel's will save it." All of the above mentioned Gospels were written long after Prophet Jesus spoke these words.

The Gospel mentioned here, Muslims believe, is the Ingeel as it was given to Prophet Jesus, and the fact that Prophet Jesus speaks and refers to the Gospel affirms this belief. The Gospel of Prophet Jesus would consist of his teachings and commandments which he received from God through the Holy Spirit – or Angel Gabriel. In John 14:24 it states "He who does not love me does not keep my words; and the word which you hear is not Mine, but the Father's who sent me." This verse is clear that Jesus Christ was referring to the word given to him by God and he asked the followers to keep his word. Similarly, John 12:47

Chapter 5: Aal-E-Imran (The Family of Imran)

states: "If anyone hears my sayings and does not keep them, I do not judge him; for I did not come to judge the world, but to save the world." He continues in verse 48, "He, who rejects me and does not receive my sayings, has one who judges him; the word I spoke is what will judge him at the last day." Prophet Jesus' continuous use of phrases like "My words" and "My sayings" implies the presence of a hidden Gospel within the Gospel. Another passage that requires Prophet Jesus' followers to adhere to his words is found in John 8:31. It states, "So Jesus was saying to those Jews who had believed Him, "If you continue in my word, then you are truly disciples of mine." Here we notice that Prophet Jesus is conditionally asserting that his true disciples will be those who follow his words.

This is corroborated by John 5:28 which states, "Truly, truly, I say to you, he who hears my word and believes Him who sent me, has eternal life, and does not come into judgment, but has passed out of death into life." These passages confirm that people who obey Prophet Jesus' words and believe in the one true God that sent him would have eternal life. On the other hand, we actually see the consequences of those who do not. In Mark 8:28, Prophet Jesus makes a point to admonish those who would be ashamed of him and his words that they would face punishment on the Day of Judgment. It says, "And for whoever is ashamed of me and my words in this adulterous and sinful generation, the Son of Man will also be ashamed of him…" From these scriptural passages, we see the emphasis on keeping and preserving his words and the deleterious consequences of failing to do so. Any open minded Christian can see the veracity of the Muslim claim of the presence of revelation given to Prophet Jesus, namely the Ingeel. This claim is further supported by John 5:46-47 which states, "For if you believed Moses you would believe me, for he wrote about me. But if you do not believe his writings, how will you believe my words?" Verse 47 is categorically clear and compels one to accept the notion that Prophet Jesus was given revelation. In this verse, Prophet Jesus is equating the disbelief of Moses' writings to that of his words. By this comparison we know that Prophet Jesus was referring to the divine revelation that he had received from God as did Prophet Moses. The Quran teaches that both Moses and Jesus were given divine scriptures in the form of the Torah and the Ingeel respectively. The idea that Prophet Jesus was given a holy scripture is not part of any Christian belief. Ironically, this is an article of faith for Muslims revealed to Prophet Muhammad. Prophet Muhammad did not have access to such knowledge as he did not know how to read. In addition, some skeptics have accused Prophet Muhammad of copying Biblical texts. The fact is that the existence of the Ingeel (revelation given to Jesus) is nowhere to be found in Christian theology or in any Christian writings. This is exclusively a part of Islamic belief validating the claim that Prophet Muhammad did not copy but received knowledge divinely. Additionally, the Quran provides specific details of events that are not found in the Bible. A superb example comes from the story of the birth of Mary. The Quran says in Surah 3:

> "A woman of Imran said, 'My Lord, I devote what is in my womb exclusively to the service of God; so accept this from me, for You are the all-hearing, all-knowing.' Then when she gave birth to her, she said, 'My Lord, I have given birth to a girl,' though God knew better what she bore—'and the male is not like the female. And I have named her Mary; and I commend her and her progeny to Your protection from Satan the accursed.' Her Lord accepted her, with a gracious reception, and caused her to grow up beautifully, and entrusted her to Zacharias. Whenever Zacharias went to her in her private chamber, he found supplies with her. He said, 'Mary, where do you get this?' She said, 'It is from God; for God provides for whomever God will, beyond any accounting.' There Zacharias prayed to his Lord. He said, 'My Lord, grant me good progeny from You; for you hear prayer.' Then the angels called him while he was standing there praying in his room, saying 'God gives you glad tidings of John, verifying a word from God, noble, chaste; a prophet, one of the righteous.' He said, 'My Lord, how can I have a son, as I am already old, and my wife is barren?' 'Thus does God do what God wills.' He said, 'My Lord, give me a sign.' 'Your sign is that you shall not speak to anyone for three days, except by signals. And remember your Lord a lot, and glorify God in the evening and the morning.' And the angels said, 'O Mary, God has chosen you and purified you, chosen you over the women of all peoples. Mary, obey your Lord devoutly, worship, and bow in prayer with those bowing in prayer.' That is from communications of the unseen, which We intimate to you. You were not with them when they were casting lots to decide which of them would support Mary, and you were not with them when they were arguing. The angels said, 'O Mary, God gives you good news of a word from God, named the Messiah, Jesus Son of

Mary, honored in the world and the hereafter, and one of the intimates of God. And he will speak to the people in infancy and maturity, and will be one of the righteous.' She said, 'My Lord! How can I have a son, when no man has touched me?' 'Thus does God create at will; when God decides on something, God simply says to it, "Be!" and it is. And God will teach him scripture and wisdom, and the Torah and the Gospel, and to be an emissary to the Children of Israel: "I have come to you with a sign from your Lord. I will make you a figure of a bird out of clay, and breathe into it, whereat it will become a bird, with God's permission. And I heal the blind and the leprous, and revive the dead, with God's permission. And I tell you what you consume and what you keep in your homes. Surely there is a sign in that for you, if you are believers. And verifying the Torah before me, and to legitimize for you some of what had been forbidden you, I have come to you with a sign from your Lord. So be conscious of God and obey me. It is God that is my Lord and your Lord, so serve God; this is a straight path."' Then when Jesus perceived atheism among them, he said, 'Who will be my allies on the way to God?' The disciples said, 'We are allies of God. We believe in God; witness that we surrender to God.' 'Our Lord, we believe in what You have revealed, and we follow the emissary; so record us among the witnesses.' Yet they plotted, but God plotted too; and God is the best of the plotters. God said, 'Jesus, I will take you unto Myself, and I will elevate you to Me, and clear you of those who scoff, and place those who follow you above those who scoff until the day of resurrection. Then you all will return to Me, and I will judge among you in matters on which you disagree. And as for those who scoff, I will punish them with severe punishment in the world and the hereafter, and they will have no saviors. And as for those who believe and do good works, God will pay them their rewards. And God does not love wrongdoers. That is what We tell you of the signs and the wise admonition.' Jesus was to God like Adam was: God created him from dust, then said, 'Be,' and he was." (Surah 3:35-59)

Christ Jesus, The Son of Mary: A Muslim Perspective

These particular passages were revealed unto Prophet Muhammad in Medina in the ninth year of the Muslim calendar (632 C.E.). The circumstances that existed in Medina at the time when these verses were revealed are interesting. After God had returned the holy city of Mecca back to the Muslims in 631 C.E., several regional powers in Arabia took notice of the growing Muslim presence. Keep in mind that Mecca was a stronghold of the pagan Arabs, and when Prophet Muhammad took over the city peacefully and without engaging in battle shocked them. Soon afterwards, a Christian community in Najran (a city between Mecca and Yemen) took notice and sent a diplomatic delegation to Medina. The king of Najran sent a group of priests and bishops to inquire about this "new religion" coming from the Arabs. The religious delegation came to Medina and spent seven to ten days with Prophet Muhammad. During this time, Prophet Muhammad received these passages from Angel Gabriel and some of the delegates were moved by what they had heard. As a result, they did not seriously challenge the authority and truthfulness of Prophet Muhammad like the pagan Arabs and the Jewish tribes did. Unlike the pagan Arabs and the Jewish tribes who had fought against the Muslims, the Christian delegation from Najran left Medina having established ecumenical relations. Although the delegates left as Christians, they were indelibly impressed with the Prophet and the revelation they had heard. In fact, a few delegates openly recognized his prophet hood and requested a few learned Muslims to accompany them back to Najran. Prophet Muhammad accepted their request and sent with them a few Muslims to teach Islam. Let us examine these passages that only Muslims and Christians share pertaining to a common belief in the Messiah and his family. You will come to know that Islam provides more details that we can learn from.

To begin our discussion of Verse 35, God reveals the birth of Mary, and ironically, the Quran is the only text that discusses this glorious event. This again substantiates the truthfulness of Prophet Muhammad because this information has never appeared in any tradition, written or oral, including Christian ones. In the verse we learn that Mary's mother, a pious woman, decided to dedicate her unborn child for the care and service of the Holy Temple in Jerusalem. It is believed that Mary's father Imran who passed away prior to her birth had priestly responsibilities in the Temple. Thus, Mary's mother desired that her child maintain the family tradition of being the caretaker of the Temple. Once again Surah 3:35 states, **"A woman of Imran said, 'My Lord, I devote what is in my womb exclusively to the service of God; so accept this from me, for You are the all-hearing, all-knowing,"**

But when the child was born, Mary's mother was shocked to learn that God had given her a female child which is not what she was expecting when she made the promise. She presumed that the unborn child would be a male and that he would be the caretaker of the Temple. Her preference for a boy was so that he, like his father, would serve the Holy Temple. The statement **"and the male is not like the female,"** is illustrative and has been interpreted in a few ways. The first interpretation is that God is speaking these words and affirming that there are natural differences between men and women. The second interpretation is that these are the words of Mary's mother and she expressed her concern that females could not serve the Holy Temple like males due to Jewish patriarchic customs. For example, women in Jewish law are unclean during their monthly menstrual cycles whereby anything or anyone that they touch becomes unclean. As such, Mary's mother believed that the male child would be better suited for the special services of the Holy Temple. However, her mother failed to realize that, **"God knew better what she bore,"** God knew that the female child is best because he has chosen her, and from her God will soon reveal some great signs of His power. Surah 3:36 follows, **"Then when she gave birth to her, she said, 'My Lord, I have given birth to a girl,' though God knew better what she bore—'and the male is not like the female."**

Despite this realization, Mary's mother is true to her oath and gives Mary for the sake of God. Before releasing Mary she offers a prayer for her: **"And I have named her Mary; and I commend her and her progeny to Your protection from Satan the accursed.'"** Seeing the dedication of the mother, God accepted and chose Mary for the glorious purpose for which she has been chosen, namely the birth of a great prophet. Since God chose her He made special arrangements for her and assigned Prophet Zachariah as her caretaker. Surah 3:37: **"Her Lord accepted her, with a gracious reception, and caused her to grow up beautifully, and entrusted her to Zacharias."** Recognizing the unique and special circumstances of her birth and being the daughter of Imran, people fought over the right to be her caretaker in the Holy Temple. So in Verse 43, we are told that they cast arrows to determine who will be assigned for Mary's care. Although the parties disputed the outcome, Prophet Zachariah was selected to be Mary's caretaker.

There might be some skepticism regarding the casting of arrows for such a sacred purpose. The simple response is that God had assigned Prophet Zachariah through His infinite knowledge and His will and power compelled the result of the arrows in favor of Prophet Zachariah. The reason for assigning Mary's care to a prophet demonstrates that she was someone very special and her upbringing needed to reflect this reality. Moreover, Prophet Zachariah was also an uncle of Mary which made the bond between them even stronger. Prophet Zachariah being assigned for Mary's care was surely a blessing for him. We read in verse 37, **"Whenever Zacharias went to her in her private chamber, he found supplies with her. He said, 'Mary, where do you get this?' She said, 'It is from God; for God provides for whomever God will, beyond any accounting.'** After seeing this miracle which was the byproduct of a righteous child, Prophet Zachariah began to petition God for a child of his own. Before we examine those verses, a thought comes to mind regarding the sustenance that Mary received. Muslim scholars believe that fruits, both seasonal and non-seasonal, were brought by angels. This is worthwhile to mention because a similar miraculous event occurs with Prophet Jesus.

So that God bestows a righteous child, Prophet Zachariah prays earnestly as mentioned in verse 38, **"There Zacharias prayed to his Lord. He said, 'My Lord, grant me good progeny from You; for you hear prayer."** In verse 39 God accepts the prayer and announces through his angels that Prophet Zachariah will have a son and his name shall be Yahya (John the Baptist). The verse makes clear that John the Baptist will be noble, chaste, and will be a prophet and among the righteous. Before God describes his character, God states the purpose and mission of John the Baptist, namely, **"verifying a word from God."** Muslims believe that this is referring to Prophet Jesus. Moreover, both Muslims and Christians agree that John the Baptist was sent to announce and witness the coming of the Messiah. In Mark 1:2, it is stated, "As it is written in Isaiah the prophet: 'Behold, I send my messenger ahead of you, who will prepare your way."

I find two things significant in verse 39. God chose to send a prophet, John the Baptist, whose conception is miraculous--as we will read--to announce and witness the coming of another prophet who is also born miraculously. Since God has a purpose and meaning for His actions we must believe that His choice of John the Baptist is most appropriate to witness the coming of a word from God. This leads to my second point. It is very important to recognize that in verse 39 God did not use the name of Prophet Jesus but declared the way he would be created. Muslims believe that Prophet Jesus was created by a word from God and this word was **"Be!"** We will discuss this in detail at another appropriate time, but notice that Muslims also refer to Prophet Jesus as the word of God. Surah 3:39 **"Then the angels called him while he was standing there praying in his room,**

Chapter 5: Aal-E-Imran (The Family of Imran)

saying 'God gives you glad tidings of John, verifying a word from God, noble, chaste; a prophet, one of the righteous.'"

In verse 40 Prophet Zachariah questioned, "**My Lord, how can I have a son, as I am already old, and my wife is barren?**" This question of Prophet Zachariah is not indicative of his disbelief as suggested in the first chapter of the Gospel of Luke. Rather, it is a sincere question of how it will come to pass. How is he going to have a son when he is old and his wife is barren? Will he and his wife become youthful? Will he have to take another wife? Or, will a child be given to them? This is not a question of doubt by Prophet Zachariah given that he just prayed for a son and was informed that his request would be soon granted. Also, as a prophet of God, Prophet Zachariah knows how God provided Prophet Abraham with children at his old age. And he has a clear and immediate example in Mary who was also conceived by parents of old age. Moreover, God responds, **"Thus does God do what God wills,"** reinforcing God's commitment and His might to achieve that which He desires. Thus, in light of such reasoning, Muslims would reject the disparaging remarks in Luke 1:20 in which Prophet Zachariah was punished by Angel Gabriel for his disbelief. We will discuss the actual punishment shortly. The actual verse (verse 40) states, "**He said, 'My Lord, how can I have a son, as I am already old, and my wife is barren?' 'Thus does God do what God wills'.**"

Having been informed that his petition was granted by God, Prophet Zachariah in verse 41 requested a sign to let him know that a miracle was pending. God informs him that he will not be able to speak to anyone for three days except by gestures. The Quran states that Prophet Zachariah did not speak for three days as a sign from God to notify that a miracle was taking place. However, Luke after his research shares the only New Testament account for Prophet Zachariah and he asserted that Prophet Zachariah was mute until John the Baptist was born. This is referenced in Luke 1:20, "And behold, you shall be silent and unable to speak until the day when these things take place, because you did not believe my words, which will be fulfilled in their proper time." This was done as a punishment because Prophet Zachariah questioned God's authority. As a consequence, Angel Gabriel turned him into a mute until the birth of John the Baptist. Here, I believe the Bible is inconsistent because Prophet Zachariah is punished as his questioning is seen as unbelief. But the same type of questioning by Abraham and Sarah or the questioning by Mary did not result in God's punishment. In Luke 1:34 Mary questions Angel Gabriel, "How can this be, since I am a virgin"? Prophet Abraham raises the same questions in Genesis 17, "Then Abraham fell on his face and laughed, and said in his heart, "Will a child be born to a man one hundred years old? And will Sarah, who is ninety years old, bear a child (17:17)?" Also Sarah in Genesis 18 asks, "And the LORD said to Abraham, 'Why did Sarah laugh, saying, 'Shall I indeed bear a child, when I am so old (18:13)?" In all three cases, God does not punish any of them.

Thus, Muslims do not believe that Prophet Zachariah was punished nor was he mute for the duration of his wife's pregnancy. A closer examination evinces that the account in the Bible is inconsistent. When we consider verse 13 of Luke 1 we can make a case that Prophet Zachariah must have told Elizabeth that the name of the child will be John, as conveyed through Angel Gabriel. Luke 1:13 states, "But the angel said to him, 'Do not be afraid, Zachariah, for your petition has been heard and your wife Elizabeth will bear you a son, and you will give him the name John." Therefore, the assertion that it was Elizabeth who came up with the name, especially since the name John had not been used in her family, is improbable. In Luke 1:60-61 it states, "But his mother answered and said, 'No indeed; but he shall be called John.' And they said to her, 'There is no one among your relatives who is called by that name.'" We must conclude that Prophet Zachariah told the name to Elizabeth prior to the birth of John the Baptist and not at his circumcision as proffered in Luke. Luke 1:63 says, "And he asked for a tablet and wrote as follows, "His name is John." And they were all astonished." At minimum, this seems to be a contradiction since God names the child John but the credit is being given to Elizabeth.

Also, it is more likely that Prophet Zachariah was not mute for nine months as he had priestly responsibilities in the Temple. Conversely, the Quran states that God ordered Prophet Zachariah to engage in the remembrance of God as an expression of gratitude for the miracle that is about to take place. Surah 3:41, **"And remember your Lord a lot, and glorify God in the evening and the morning."** This is what a prophet of God should be doing especially when God promised the blessing of a child who will become a prophet.

Clearly, there are significant differences between Luke's account of these events and the Quranic position. These differences at first glance may seem trivial but they highlight how prophets are viewed in the two traditions. The honor and respect of prophets is central to Muslim belief, and without this credibility, their message is compromised. Moreover, by juxtaposing the Quranic text and the Biblical verses we are in a better position to reach certain conclusions. And let it be the reader to decide upon the truth. If an inconsistency exists as the one in the

Bible mentioned above, the reader must determine what accounts are more believable. Surah 3:41 states, "**He said, 'My Lord, give me a sign.' 'Your sign is that you shall not speak to anyone for three days, except by signals. And remember your Lord a lot, and glorify God in the evening and the morning.**"

In verse 42, we see that God has sent an angel to inform Mary that she has been chosen above the women of all nations and that God has purified her. We will read for why she was chosen in subsequent verses. But in verse 42, we know that God has kept her pure. God magnified her spirituality because she was raised by Prophet Zachariah and grew up in the Holy Temple. Also, God kept her pure in the physical realm as she was not capable of any immorality. God protected her from Satan and temptation as requested by Mary's mother after her birth. This becomes an issue when the unfaithful Jews accused Mary of a grave sin. But the truth is manifest in the statement, "God has chosen thee and purified thee." It may seem surprising to some Christians to see the level of love, honor and respect that Muslims have for Lady Mary and her high status in Islam. In this vein, consider two additional points. First, Surah 19 is named "Mary." This may seem insignificant but of the 114 Surahs in the Holy Quran, there are no Surahs named for Prophets Moses, Jesus, Adam, Solomon, Zachariah or Yahya. Secondly, there is only one woman mentioned in the entire Quran by name and that is Lady Mary. All other women are mentioned by relationships. In other words, God refers to the various women as wives of ... (wife of Abraham, wife of Noah, etc.). Lady Mary is revered in the same way as are holy prophets. As such, in verse 43 God commands Mary to worship Him in a manner that befits God's Lordship (i.e. through bowing and prostrating). By this injunction, we know that more obedience is expected of the chosen ones. Since she has been chosen by God, He commands her that she should increase her devotion and surrender to Him by prostrating with other worshipers. Phrased simply, her being chosen does not preclude her from worshipping God just like other faithful servants. The fact that Mary prays with others is humbling for her, and more importantly, the people she prays with will hopefully be able to attest to her noble character when Prophet Jesus is born. Thus, in verse 43 God commands her to be devoted to Him. Verse 44 specifies why she has been chosen. However, verse 43 ends by God reminding the Christian delegates from Najran that these passages detailing the accounts of Mary and her family were well before the Prophet's time. It is God who has revealed the knowledge onto Prophet Muhammad and the Quran provides facts that are not found in any Christian writings. The circumstances of the birth of Mary, the reason for Prophet Zachariah's petition for a son, and the dispute among people who wished to be the caretaker of Mary and their casting of lots all appear in the Quran alone. Clearly Prophet Muhammad received divine revelation and is a true prophet of God.

Surah 3:42-46 are as follows:

"And the angels said, 'O Mary, God has chosen you and purified you, chosen you over the women of all peoples. Mary, obey your Lord devoutly, worship, and bow in prayer with those bowing in prayer.' That is from communications of the unseen, which We intimate to you. You were not with them when they were casting lots to decide which of them would support Mary, and you were not with them when they were arguing. The angels said, 'O Mary, God gives you good news of a word from God, named the Messiah, Jesus Son of Mary, honored in the world and the hereafter, and one of the intimates of God. And he will speak to the people in infancy and maturity, and will be one of the righteous.'"

In verse 45 we read that the angels brought the following news, **"The angels said, 'O Mary, God gives you good news of a word from God, named the Messiah, Jesus Son of Mary, honored in the world and the hereafter, and one of the intimates of God."** As mentioned earlier, Muslims refer to Prophet Jesus as the **"Word from God"** because of the method that God used to bring Prophet Jesus into being. The word that God spoke was **"Be,"** and with this decree brings forth which He desires. God simply uttered **"Be,"** and Prophet Jesus was conceived. Moreover, as God created him by His word, God names the child, Christ Jesus the son of Mary. The verse adds that he will be honored in the world and will be in the Hereafter as one of the nearest to God. Even prior to Jesus' birth, God informs Mary that her son will have an eminent place in both realms of existence.

We then read in verse 46 that Prophet Jesus will speak to the people as an infant and in maturity. There are two points of clarification concerning verse 46 which states: **"And he will speak to the people in infancy and maturity, and will be one of the righteous."** As we will read in Surah 19:27-33, Muslims believe that one of the miracles of Prophet Jesus was that he spoke as an infant. Although this will be developed later, a brief summation of what happened may prove to be helpful. When Mary brought baby Jesus to the people they were

Chapter 5: Aal-E-Imran (The Family of Imran)

shocked to see her with a child. In such a situation, people will think the worst when an unmarried young woman appears with a baby. Jewish law placed a primacy on family honor and harsh punishments for wrongful acts. Consequently, God gave Prophet Jesus the power of speech as a newborn so that the people could recognize that the child is holy and from God. This miracle comforted and cleansed the believer's hearts, but the disbelievers accused Mary of a grave sin.

The second point concerning verse 46 is the statement that Prophet Jesus will speak in maturity, or in the Arabic "Kahulath." The word Kahulath describes a stage of life beginning approximately from 35-45 years of age during which maturity, prudence, and wisdom begin to manifest themselves in a person. However, being able to speak at this age is not unusual and for God to mention that Prophet Jesus will speak in maturity may seem superfluous. But of course every word in the Quran serves a purpose and contains wisdom. Thus, Muslim scholars believe that this may be a reference to the second coming of Prophet Jesus as he had not yet reached the Kahulath stage when he was raised up into heaven.

Having heard the news of a son, Mary's obvious question was, **"My Lord! How can I have a son, when no man has touched me?"** Again, this question is not indicative of disbelief but a lack of understanding at the human level. What does the phrase **"good news of a word from God"** truly mean? The creation of human beings by God's word (**Be**) had not been done since Prophet Adam. Also, observe that she addresses the question to God saying, **"My Lord!"** This is important so that we can know that Mary is not calling the angels Lord. Since Angel Gabriel is only a deliverer of messages from God, Mary poses her question to God directly. Hence, God responds to Mary's inquiry through the angels and he said, **"Thus does God create at will; when God decides on something, God simply says to it, 'Be!' and it is."**

This is the Muslim account of the Immaculate Conception. Although some Christians have doubts concerning the Immaculate Conception, the Quran has preserved it and the belief in this supernatural event is a part of Islamic faith. One needs to understand that God has created the heavens and the earth and everything in between. He then established certain natural laws and principles that govern His creation. But He being the sovereign God is not subject to these laws because, after all, He created them. Thus, if God creates human life by His command in order to fulfill the divine plan, then it should not be a cause for disbelief. Moreover, we know that the word **"Be"** was used when God created the universe(s). Genesis verses 1, 3, 6, 9, 14, 21, and 24, are referred to as the Creation Verses. God says *"Be"* for the purpose of bringing things into existence. In each case God says, "Let there *be*..." Genesis 1:1 states "God created the heavens and the earth." Genesis 1:3 says "Let there *be* light," 1:6 says "Let there *be* an expanse in the midst of the waters," 1:9 declares, "Let the waters below the heavens *be* gathered into one place, and let the dry land appear," 1:14 is "Then God said, 'Let there *be* lights in the expanse of the heavens to separate the day from the night, and let them *be* for signs and for seasons and for days and years.'"

Therefore, Muslims believe that the command word **"Be"** was said by God to create Prophet Jesus Christ and it is for this reason that Muslims refer to him as the word from God. Interestingly, in Luke 1:38 we see that Mary responds to Gabriel and states, "Behold, the bond slave of the Lord; may it be done to me according to *your word*." Here we have Mary identifying and accepting God's decree. This decree evolved into the Christian adoption of *Logos*, the Greek pagan concept of "the word." However, the Christian-pagan concept of the *Logos* as God is absolutely unacceptable for Muslims. It is unacceptable for two main reasons. First, the *Logos* is not divine as suggested in the Gospel of John 1:1-2 because it challenges the fundamental Jewish and Muslim principle of the belief in the one true God. John 1:1-2 states "In the beginning was the Word and the Word was with God, and the Word was God. He was in the beginning with God." This verse calls into question the singularity and oneness of God. How can something be with God and be God at the same time? Similarly, Jesus sitting at the right hand of God conveys that God and Jesus are separate and not one. If Jesus and God are indeed one, as Christians purport, then this belief goes against the first commandment contradicting the monotheistic belief that there is only one true God. The second reason that Muslims reject the *Logos* being divine is because it was a pagan concept that was adopted by the Christians in order that they may convert the Greek Gentiles. The concept of the *Logos* predates Prophet Jesus and can be traced back to Heraclitus and the Greeks. The *Logos* was a divine entity that helped them make sense of the physical earthly existence. Perhaps the early Christians who were seen as ignorant by the Greek Gentiles adopted the mysterious pagan concept of the *Logos* and wrongfully applied it to Prophet Jesus.

Early Christians also adopted pagan holy days to fit Christian traditions. One good example is the celebration of Prophet Jesus Christ's birthday. On December 25th the Romans had a celebration for the rebirth of the sun called Sol Invictus but when Christians came along they replaced the pagan festival with the birthday of Prophet Jesus. These are pagan concepts and traditions that have been

Chapter 5: Aal-E-Imran (The Family of Imran)

incorporated to make Christianity palatable to the Romans. The *Logos* being divine is inconsistent with the teachings of monotheism. However, the word becoming flesh (John 1:14) is consistent with the Muslim belief that God created Prophet Jesus by His word. This was clearly established in Surah 3 verse 45.

In verse 48 God states, **"And God will teach him scripture and wisdom, and the Torah and the Gospel."** This verse makes it evident that Prophet Jesus as well as other prophets received their wisdom and scripture from the Lord. It is given to them in order that they may accomplish the duty that all prophets are assigned, namely, to bring the people to the path of God. The fact that he was taught the scriptures demonstrates that he was not divine. In Luke 2:52, we learn that the angels were ministering to Prophet Jesus and through this learning he was able to increase his knowledge and wisdom. Luke 2:52 "And Jesus kept increasing in wisdom and stature, and in favor with God and men." God is the epitome of perfection and is beyond increase or diminution. It was God through His angels who would teach Prophet Jesus knowledge of the Torah, and this is why he was able to speak to the Jews as "one having the authority." This is confirmed by John 7:15 which states, "The Jews then were astonished, saying, "How has this man become learned, having never been educated?"

Both biblical verses demonstrate that Prophet Jesus was taught knowledge of the Torah and Ingeel. In Surah 3 verse 3, we discussed that Prophet Jesus was given the Ingeel which is empirically supported by the four Gospels. However, the question can be raised – what do Muslims say about the New Testament? Here, the Muslim position is that it is not the Ingeel given to Prophet Jesus but does contain some core truths that are part of the Ingeel. In essence, we believe in those passages that are confirmed by the Quran or that which do not contradict its teachings. Let me illustrate both types of texts and provide examples. Muslims accept the passages of the New Testament which the Quran confirms – i.e. Prophet Jesus' miraculous birth, his prophet hood, his miracles, and his claim of returning to earth in the final days. However, the following things are rejected: the notion that he was the son of God, crucifixion and burial, resurrection, and living for forty days before ascending into heaven. Because these beliefs contradict the Quran, Muslims would say that they are untrue and that such words are falsely attributed to him as he was an obedient servant of God. Merely by someone writing down such words decades after his ascension do not make them credible. One must examine these assertions to determine if they comport to his other teachings. For example, one of the most frequently discussed themes in the New Testament is this notion that "The Kingdom of God is at hand." Prophet

Jesus is quoted as saying that "the Kingdom of God is at hand and this generation will not die until these things come to pass." Let us examine a detailed passage where Jesus prophesizes many events. Luke 21:23-35 states,

> Woe to those who are pregnant and those who are nursing babies in those days; for there will be great distress upon the land and wraith to this people; and they will fall by the edge of the sword, and will be led captive into all the nations; and Jerusalem will be trampled underfoot by the Gentiles until the times of the Gentiles are fulfilled. There will be signed in sun and moon and stars, and on the earth dismay among nations, in perplexity at the roaring of the sea and the waves, men fainting from fear and the expectation of the things which are coming upon the world; for the powers of the heavens will be shaken. Then they will see *The Son of Man coming in a cloud with power and great glory*. But when these things begin to take place, straighten up and lift up your heads, because your redemption is drawing near.' Then he told them a parable: 'Behold the fig tree and all the trees; as soon as they put forth leaves, you see it and know for yourselves that summer is now near. So you also, when you see these things happening, recognize that the kingdom of God is near. Truly I say to you, *this generation will not pass away until all things take place*. Heaven and earth will not be weighted down with dissipation and drunkenness and the worries of life, and that day will not come on you suddenly like a trap; for it will come upon all those who dwell on the face of all the earth.

As some of the prophecies were occurring, the Apostles and most Christians were convinced that Jesus Christ was coming in their lifetime as he promised them in Luke 9:27 and they believed it until their last days. Sadly, they are dead and yet two thousand years later the Kingdom of God is still not at hand. Therefore, Muslims would reject the notion that he misled his followers by making such statements that would give his people false hope. Another example of a statement that is attributed to Prophet Jesus is in Matthew 12:40 which states, "for just as Jonah was three days and three nights in the belly of the sea monster, so will the Son of Man be three days and three nights in the heart of the earth." This statement could not have been attributed to Prophet Jesus because a closer reading of the Gospels leads us to question its plausibility. Prophet Jesus was

Chapter 5: Aal-E-Imran (The Family of Imran)

crucified Friday afternoon and was resurrected Sunday afternoon. If we calculate the time according to the Jewish calendar, a new day begins after sunset, and thus the statement "three days and three nights" cannot be accurate. Consider the following: Friday at sunset to Saturday at sunset is one day, and Saturday at sunset to Sunday afternoon is not even a full day. According to a simple calculation, this is not even two days and two nights! Christians cannot dismiss this statement as a mere metaphor in order to justify this falsehood. Hence, Muslims reject this statement being attributed to Prophet Jesus. These types of inconsistencies lead many Christians and Muslims to doubt the claim of authenticity and infallibility of the Bible. Despite these shortcomings, Muslims nevertheless embrace the universal truths espoused in the Bible and believe that both Jews and Christians are People of the Book. Let us return to our examination of Surah 3.

In verse 49 we read, **"And to be an emissary to the Children of Israel: 'I have come to you with a sign from your Lord. I will make you a figure of a bird out of clay, and breathe into it, whereat it will become a bird, with God's permission. And I heal the blind and the leprous, and revive the dead, with God's permission. And I tell you what you consume and what you keep in your homes. Surely there is a sign in that for you, if you are believers."** This verse is clear and explicates who Prophet Jesus is and why he has been sent. Let us analyze this verse more closely. After revealing in verse 48 that God will teach Prophet Jesus the Torah and the Ingeel, in verse 49 we read that He will appoint Jesus Christ as a messenger to the Children of Israel. Muslims believe that Prophet Jesus was sent only to the Jewish people and no one else, and this is confirmed by the Bible. In Matthew 15:24 Prophet Jesus states, "I was sent only to the lost sheep of the house of Israel." Moreover, in Matthew 10:5-6 it states, "These twelve Jesus sent out after instruction them: 'Do not go in the way of the Gentiles, and do not enter any city of Samaritans; but rather go to the lost sheep of the house of Israel...'" He also taught his disciples to only minister to the Jews. In addition, he taught in synagogues, told his followers to obey the commandments of Prophet Moses, observed Jewish rituals (i.e. Passover), and was called The King of the Jews. Such realities are ignored by most Christians who believe that Prophet Jesus was sent to the world. Again, Muslims believe that he was sent exclusively to the Jews and the reason for this becomes clear when we understand why he was sent in verse 50. Beforehand, a few additional thoughts on verse 49 come to mind.

First, it must be clearly understood that any miracle is the act of God and it is His doing and prophets are but the vessels by which God performs His signs.

The miracles that Prophet Jesus performed are no exception and he attributed his miracles to God's will. The fact that God performed the miracles through Jesus Christ is supported by the Apostle Peter in Acts 2:22 which states, "Men of Israel, listen to these words: Jesus the Nazarene, a man attested to you by God with miracles and wonders and signs which God performed through Him in your midst." Moreover we have already learned in John 12:47 that Prophet Jesus did not do anything of his own initiative which would certainly include any of his miracles. That being said, is it not out of the ordinary to label Prophet Jesus anything but a prophet and servant of God? Secondly, we had discussed earlier that God had given Prophet Jesus clear signs and in verse 49 we are informed about a few of them. Although healing the lepers, the blind, and raising the dead are mentioned in the New Testament, the other two are not. There is no mention in the New Testament that Prophet Jesus made from clay a bird-like figure and breathed into it; and the clay figure became a live bird. Interestingly, there is a mention of Prophet Jesus using clay to heal a blind man. In John 9:11 the blind man states, "The man who is called Jesus made clay, and anointed my eyes, and said to me, 'Go Siloam and wash;' so I went away and washed, and I received sight." Thus, if he can heal a blind man using clay, then it should not surprise anyone if he performed the Quranic miracle mentioned above. There is nonetheless an obscure reference in the gospel of Thomas in which Prophet Jesus made twelve sparrows out of clay which flew away after he clapped his hands. This is not the Quranic depiction but the essence is the same.

Finally, the New Testament does not have any record that Prophet Jesus told the people detailed information of what each one ate and stored in their homes. There is, however, an acknowledgment in the Gospel of John of additional miracles that were not documented. In John 21:25 the following passage appears: "And there are also many other things which Jesus did, which if they were written in detail, I suppose that even the world itself would not contain the books that would be written." By virtue of the Quran discussing miracles that are not mentioned in the Bible, this should not lead one to cavalierly conclude that such miracles were not performed. The sole purpose of miracles that Prophet Jesus performed was to demonstrate the truthfulness of him being a messenger of God and the Christ whom the Jews were awaiting. However, did such miracles lead people to faith? The answer can be found in Luke 10:13-15 in which Prophet Jesus condemned those cities that observed the miracles and still rejected faith. Luke 10: 13-15 states, "Woe to you, Chorazin! Woe to you, Bethsaida! For if the miracles had been performed in Tyre and Sidon which occurred in you, they would have repented long ago, sitting in sack cloth and ashes. But it will be more

Chapter 5: Aal-E-Imran (The Family of Imran)

tolerable for Tyre and Sidon in the judgment than for you. And you, Caprnaum, will not be exalted to heaven, will you? You will be brought down to Hades!" When we read his lamentation, it is disheartening because Muslims believe that he was sent for their benefit. In verse 50 it states, **"And verifying the Torah before me, and to legitimize for you some of what had been forbidden you, I have come to you with a sign from your Lord. So be conscious of God and obey me."'** In this verse it is clear that Prophet Jesus was sent to confirm the law and make lawful things which were forbidden at that time. Essentially, he was sent to facilitate and ease the erstwhile constraints. No one can deny the austere restrictions that were placed upon the Jewish people under the law (Torah). Muslims believe that those restrictions were made because of the disobedience of the Sons of Jacob. Hence, God responded with more instructions that set strict parameters around their behavior such that their lives became burdensome. Ultimately, God in His infinite mercy sent Prophet Jesus to lift some of the laws so that the Jewish people could live more freely. We are not certain about those restrictions that were lifted because we do not have the Ingeel (The Gospel of Prophet Jesus). However, the New Testament does indicate some relaxation with regard to a few Jewish Laws. For example, there was no work to be done on the Sabbath under Jewish law. However, Prophet Jesus taught by example that certain types of work could be done for the sake of goodness. In Luke 6:1-3 Prophet Jesus along with his Apostles picked wheat from the field to feed themselves. According to this passage in Luke, "Now it happened that He was passing through some grain fields on a Sabbath; and His disciples were picking the heads of grain, rubbing them in their hands, and eating the grain. But some of the Pharisees said, "Why do you do what is not lawful on the Sabbath?" And Jesus answered, "Have you not even read what David did when he was hungry, he and those who were with him."

In another example, Prophet Jesus healed a man's arm on the Sabbath. In Matthew 12:12 it states, "How much more valuable then is a man than a sheep? So then, it is lawful to do good on the Sabbath." Finally, it would also appear that Prophet Jesus did away with the ritual hand washing that the Jews had to perform before eating. In Mark 7:5 it reads, "The Pharisees and the scribes asked him, "Why do your disciples not walk according to the tradition of the elders, but eat their bread with impure hands?" It may be these types of restrictions that could have been lifted, but no one really knows since the Ingeel is no longer with us. More germane to Muslims is that Prophet Jesus was sent as a blessing. Christ means "the blessed one" who came to make the lives of the Jewish people more in line with what God had originally intended for them. From this lens, we can understand Matthew 5:17 which states, "Do not think that I came to abolish the Law or the Prophets; I did not come to abolish but to fulfill." These verses confirm that the law was going to be amended but not abolished.

Keep in mind that the Jewish faith was in the hands of very corrupt people who used their knowledge of the law and authority for personal gains. Their exploitation of the law and their authority made religion a burden for the people. Moreover, the law which was codified in Hebrew was not understood by most Jews living at the time of Prophet Jesus. Most of them spoke Aramaic which denied them access to the law and contributed to their subjugation to the religious authorities. Thus, God sent Prophet Jesus to the Jewish people to guide them to the correct path of God and gave Prophet Jesus the Ingeel. The Ingeel did not completely replace the Law, but amended it such that it made some things lawful which were otherwise forbidden. In my humble opinion, the Ingeel was revealed in Aramaic because it was the vernacular of those living in first-century Palestine. It is likely that God provided divine scripture to the Jewish people in their own language so that they may understand and obey its teachings. This is an important point to consider for if we believe that Prophet Jesus spoke Aramaic, as did most of his people, then we can make the argument that the Ingeel must have been in Aramaic. In fact, Surah 14:4 states, **"We never sent a messenger who did not use the language of his people to bring them clarity of understanding. And God leaves people astray at will, and guides anyone at will; and God is the almighty, supremely wise."**

The Torah was given to the Sons of Jacob nearly 1,300 years before Prophet Jesus in Hebrew. But when Prophet Jesus came most Jews could not speak Hebrew, and those that did corrupted the Jewish Law. In response, God sent Prophet Jesus with the Ingeel to correct and restore the divine law. This is the Muslim position as stated in Surah 3:50. This is also confirmed by Luke 16:16 which states "The Law and the Prophets were proclaimed until John; since that time the gospel of the kingdom of God has been preached." The verse mostly supports the Muslim claim that the Gospel replaced the Law and the Prophets. Moreover, the Gospel mentioned in Luke 16:16 cannot refer to the Gospels of the New Testament because they were written nearly twenty five to fifty years after Prophet Jesus. Hence, we can surmise that every time the word Gospel appears in the Bible, it is in reference to the Ingeel, not merely the Christian notion that the Gospel refers to the good news, the coming of Jesus Christ.

Chapter 5: Aal-E-Imran (The Family of Imran)

One last commentary on Surah 3:50 relates to the way that it ends. It ends with Prophet Jesus saying, **"I have come to you with a sign from your Lord. So be conscious of God (fear God) and obey me."** This verse declares that Prophet Jesus preached to the people about fearing God. However, most Christians today do not like to be preached to about fearing God or His wrath. This interpretation of the Bible does not conform to the Pollyanna view of Jesus coming to redeem the sins of mankind. Such a perception is not in keeping with the reality that Prophet Jesus taught the people to fear God. Think of the numerous times Prophet Jesus taught the virtue of repentance. This is a recurring theme throughout the Bible and in the sermons of Prophet Jesus. Muslims are also taught to repent and seek God's mercy and forgiveness because we are all sinners. The Quran and the Hadith (traditions of Prophet Muhammad) emphasize repentance and the importance of fearing God. The Quran teaches that God-fearing believers are the ones closest to Him. This is consistent with the statement of Lady Mary in Luke 1:50 in which she states "And his mercy is on generation after generation toward those who fear him." Luke 14:7 teaches, "I tell you then in the same way there will be more joy in heaven over one sinner who repents then over ninety-nine righteous persons who need repentance."

Also when we examine verse 50 we see Prophet Jesus telling the people to fear God and obey Him. We read in the Gospels on numerous occasions that Prophet Jesus told the people to follow him. The implication is that following the teachings of Prophet Jesus leads one to the right path. Can anyone find one instance in which Prophet Jesus taught his followers to worship him? Can anyone cite one instance where Prophet Jesus or his followers prayed to anyone except God? This is the challenge to the reader. No one will be able to locate anywhere in the Gospels either of these practices. He never taught his followers to worship him and nor did he worship anyone except God. How then can Christians call him God and worship him? If Christians claim to follow Jesus Christ, then why not worship the way he worshipped and to whom he worshipped? The claim that Prophet Jesus is anything more than a man and servant of God is contradictory to what he taught and practiced. Muslims believe that any quotations attributed to Prophet Jesus that suggested that he was God would be dismissed as fabrications. His teachings and his servitude to God overwhelmingly prove that he was obedient to God alone. How do we know that he was not more than a servant of God? The answer is in Surah 3:51 which states: **"It is God that is my Lord and your Lord, so serve God; this is a straight path."** Muslims believe Prophet Jesus taught his people to fear and worship the one true God as he worshipped Him. On many occasions, Prophet Jesus is seen worshipping God for a significant length of time. For example, Luke 5:16 says, "But Jesus himself would *often* slip away to the wilderness and pray." Prophet Jesus is also seen praying as in the verse in Luke 6:12: "He spent the whole night in *prayer to God*." These two verses sustain the truth that Prophet Jesus submitted to a greater authority than himself. The surrender to an ultimate Reality whereby the servant makes himself or herself insignificant in His presence is the essence of worship. Accordingly, Prophet Jesus is seen worshipping with his face on the ground often alone at night. Prophet Jesus worshipped God precisely as Muslims are commanded to worship, and there is no difference between his worship and our worship of God. There is the mutual recognition in Islam and in the teachings of Jesus that there is only one entity worthy of our worship. There is only one God and He is the creator and sustainer of the heavens, earth, and all else in between. He is God of us all, including Prophet Jesus as he himself declared in John 20:17: "Stop clinging to Me, for I have not yet ascended to the Father; but go to My brethren and say to them, 'I ascend to My Father and your Father, and My God and your God.'" And in Luke 18:18-19, "A ruler questioned Him, saying, 'Good Teacher, what shall I do to inherit eternal life?' And Jesus said to him, 'Why do you call me good? No one is good except God alone." These two passages are clear examples that demonstrate Prophet Jesus is not claiming to be God, and making certain that no one associates him with God.

Let us recapitulate and ponder over these important verses once again.

"The angels said, 'O Mary, God gives you good news of a word from God, named the Messiah, Jesus Son of Mary, honored in the world and the hereafter, and one of the intimates of God. And he will speak to the people in infancy and maturity, and will be one of the righteous.' She said, 'My Lord! How can I have a son, when no man has touched me?' 'Thus does God create at will; when God decides on something, God simply says to it, "Be!" and it is. And God will teach him scripture and wisdom, and the Torah and the Gospel, and to be an emissary to the Children of Israel: "I have come to you with a sign from your Lord. I will make you a figure of a bird out of clay, and breathe into it, whereat it will become a bird, with God's permission. And I heal the blind and the leprous, and revive the dead, with God's permission. And I tell you what you consume and what you keep in your homes. Surely there is a sign in that

Chapter 5: Aal-E-Imran (The Family of Imran)

for you, if you are believers. And verifying the Torah before me, and to legitimize for you some of what had been forbidden you, I have come to you with a sign from your Lord. So be conscious of God and obey me. It is God that is my Lord and your Lord, so serve God; this is a straight path.'" Then when Jesus perceived atheism among them, he said, 'Who will be my allies on the way to God?' The disciples said, 'We are allies of God. We believe in God; witness that we surrender to God.' 'Our Lord, we believe in what You have revealed, and we follow the emissary; so record us among the witnesses.' Yet they plotted, but God plotted too; and God is the best of the plotters. God said, 'Jesus, I will take you unto Myself, and I will elevate you to Me, and clear you of those who scoff, and place those who follow you above those who scoff until the day of resurrection. Then you all will return to Me, and I will judge among you in matters on which you disagree. And as for those who scoff, I will punish them with severe punishment in the world and the hereafter, and they will have no saviors. And as for those who believe and do good works, God will pay them their rewards. And God does not love wrongdoers. That is what We tell you of the signs and the wise admonition.' Jesus was to God like Adam was: God created him from dust, then said, 'Be,' and he was."

How did the Jewish people respond to Jesus' teachings despite having witnessed the clear signs and miracles that he had performed? The majority of them rejected him. However, a small minority not only accepted Prophet Jesus as the Christ but they helped him in his ministry. In verse 52 we read, **"Then when Jesus perceived atheism among them, he said, 'Who will be my allies on the way to God?' The disciples said, 'We are allies of God. We believe in God; witness that we surrender to God."** This verse makes it very clear that Prophet Jesus had true believers whom the Quran refers to as *Hawareen* which means "to return." Thus, God calls them *Hawareen* because they returned to the straight path of God. The New Testament writers refer to the followers of Prophet Jesus as disciples. They are one and the same, but the *Hawareen* are not restricted to the twelve Apostles. The help of the disciples came in the form of spreading the news that the Christ had come in the various Jewish cities surrounding Jerusalem. According to Matthew 10:5-6, "These twelve Jesus sent out after instructing them:

'Do not go in the way of the Gentiles, and do not enter any city of Samaritans; but rather go to the lost sheep of the house of Israel.'" The disciples assumed the responsibility to continue preaching to the Jews after Prophet Jesus had been lifted up into heaven. It must be forcefully emphasized that the true disciples of Prophet Jesus did not advocate the establishment of a new religion or church. However, Paul of Tarsus, after initially persecuting Christians began to preach the "Gospel of Grace" to the Gentiles after his conversion. This Gospel or Good News claimed that one no longer needed to be under the Law of Moses and nor did one need to be a Jew to be saved. This may be the widely accepted narration today, but keep in mind that this version of the truth goes against the teachings of Prophet Jesus and his orders to his disciples. Prophet Jesus prayed for his disciples in the following way: "Holy Father, keep them in Your name" (John 17:11). Despite this exalted position of the disciples, we find a new figure (Paul) who claimed to be a disciple of Jesus and yet undermined and overturned everything that Prophet Jesus taught. One of the most damaging of Paul's teachings, which contributed to the formation of a new religion (Christianity), is the abandonment of the Law (the Torah). The Law of Moses established clear parameters of acceptable and unacceptable behavior. It outlined clear injunctions and prohibitions in eating, marriage, prayer, holy customs, and, above all, penalties for unlawful actions. By keeping the law, there would have been a more substantive Jewish identity of Christianity as taught by Prophet Jesus as opposed to the development of a separate religion. It is for this reason the Catholic Church over the years felt compelled to codify clear doctrinal guidelines in the form of Catechisms, defined by Random House as "an elementary book containing a summary of the principles of the Christian religion."

However, the true followers of Prophet Jesus were believing Jews that followed Prophet Jesus and obeyed the divine revelation given to them as we will read in verse 53. These Jewish believers did not preach a new religion but simply adhered to what Prophet Jesus taught. Hence, in Verse 52 they asked Prophet Jesus to attest to the fact that they were Muslims. The verse states **"We are allies of God. We believe in God; witness that we surrender to God (we are Muslims)."** The confusion might arise why his followers would ask him to attest to them being Muslims. In the common lexicon, a Muslim is one who believes in one God and follows Prophet Muhammad. Such a person indeed would be called a Muslim. However, the word Muslim can also be used as an adjective to describe a person who surrenders to God. Therefore, anyone who accepts the teachings of the prophets and worships in the manner taught by their prophet would be called a Muslim, for they have surrendered to God. By virtue of adhering to the true

Chapter 5: Aal-E-Imran (The Family of Imran)

teachings of their messenger, they would be called Muslims. As such, when the disciples call themselves Muslims they are submitting to the command of God, and in this case to believe in one God and obey the teachings of Prophet Jesus Christ. In fact, their declaration of faith is found in Verse 53 which states, **"Our Lord, we believe in what You have revealed, and we follow the emissary; so record us among the witnesses."** In both verses 52 and 53 we see a pure and complete faith of the believers of Prophet Jesus. In Verse 52 they declare their belief in God and aspire to do the work that pleases Him. In Verse 53 they believe in the revelation given to them (the Gospel) and they follow the messenger (Prophet Jesus). These aspects are the main principles of true and complete faith. Muslims believe that followers of Prophet Jesus were true believers that were faithful to Prophet Jesus and righteous and obedient to God. According to John 17:6 Jesus says, "... they have kept Your word." Additionally, in John 17:8 Jesus continues, "For the words which You gave me I have *given to them*, and they received them and truly understood that I came forth from You, and they believed that You sent me." This verse again confirms the Muslim claim that Prophet Jesus was given revelation which he passed on to his followers.

Therefore, Muslims reject the accounts in the New Testament that portray Prophet Jesus' followers as cowardly and without faith. How can Prophet Jesus leave his ministry to unfaithful people that abandoned him in his time of need? Those disciples that denied Prophet Jesus in the Gospels were the same people led by Peter who courageously spoke against the Jewish authority in an open forum. Hence, in Acts chapters 1 and 2 Peter screams at the Jewish clergy without any fear for his life. Can this be the same Peter who denied Prophet Jesus three different times? Muslims believe not. Christians may attribute Peter's courage to him receiving the Holy Spirit. The fact is that more important than the Holy Spirit was the company of Prophet Jesus. Muslims believe they had complete faith because the Quran is clear concerning it. It is ironic that Muslims defend the faith of the disciples whereas Christians question it. Besides, John 17 is entirely devoted to the disciples being faithful, righteous, and chosen by God. John 17:6 says, "I have manifested Your name to the men whom You gave me out of the world; they were Yours and You gave them to me, and *they have kept Your word*." More importantly, Prophet Jesus prayed for them prior to his arrest by the Romans, and we must believe that his prayers were answered. However, Muslims will agree with the Christians that most of the Jewish people denied Prophet Jesus. They did so not due to their ignorance, but with full knowledge that he was the Christ. Rather, they knowingly rejected the Christ because of their pride. The Jewish authority (Sanhedrin) who had great influence among the people were losing their authority when Prophet Jesus denounced their unrighteous practices. Hence, they plotted to eliminate Prophet Jesus. In Verse 54 we learn, **"Yet they plotted, but God plotted too; and God is the best of the plotters."** In hindsight, we know what sort of plans they had in mind. They were going to kill Prophet Jesus just as their forefathers (the unbelieving Jews) had done so many times in the past. However, God also had a plan and his plans are the best. What was God's Plan? We read in Verse 55, **"God said, 'Jesus, I will take you unto Myself, and I will elevate you to Me, and clear you of those who scoff, and place those who follow you above those who scoff until the day of resurrection. Then you all will return to Me, and I will judge among you in matters on which you disagree."**

This verse reveals God's plan for Prophet Jesus which was to save him from the Jewish authority by raising him into heaven. Muslims and Christians believe that Prophet Jesus was lifted up into heaven but disagree on the timing. Christians believe that Prophet Jesus was crucified, died on the cross, was buried, rose on the third day, lived on the Earth for forty days, and then was lifted up into heaven sitting at the right hand of "the Father." By contrast, Muslims believe that Prophet Jesus was lifted up into heaven without any harm befalling him. He faced no brutal treatment at the hands of Jewish authority or the Roman soldiers. Prophet Jesus did not die nor was he nailed on the cross. There is unanimous consensus among all Muslims without exception that Prophet Jesus did not perish on the cross nor was he crucified. Surah 4:157 speaks to this matter,

> **"And on account of their saying 'We killed the Messiah Jesus, Son of Mary, messenger of God,' whereas they did not kill him, they did not crucify him, although it was made to seem thus to them. As for those who differ on this, they are certainly in doubt about it. They have no knowledge about it, only following conjecture; but they surely did not kill him."**

We will further develop this verse in chapter sixteen, but for our present purposes, the Muslim position is that Prophet Jesus was neither killed nor crucified. This is the Quranic account. But what about the Bible? I believe that the Bible confirms the Muslim position and I outline it in detail when we discuss Surah 4:157. For now, consider Luke 4:10-11 which states, "For it is written he will give his angels charge concerning you and guard you. And on their hands they will bear you up less you strike your foot against a stone." The question that requires reflection is: where were the angels who were put in charge of raising Prophet Jesus before he is harmed at the time of the crucifixion? Is not the crucifixion the most pressing occasion for angels to raise Prophet Jesus? And, this is consistent with God's plan as it was known even prior to Prophet Jesus.

One final point needs to be made regarding verse 55 on the status of those who believed in the Christ as opposed to the ones who rejected him. The verse states, "**God said, 'Jesus, I will take you unto Myself, and I will elevate you to Me, and clear you of those who scoff, and place those who follow you above those who scoff until the day of resurrection. Then you all will return to Me, and I will judge among you in matters on which you disagree.**" An important observation often overlooked is that both the followers of Prophet Jesus as well as those who rejected and plotted against him were Jews. Thus, it should be noted that God is not anti-Jewish when he displays his displeasure by punishing the disbelieving Jews. Rather, He does so because of their disobedience and rejection of faith. That being said, God has promised Prophet Jesus that his followers will be superior over those who rejected him. This was done by God as a punishment to the Jews till the Day of Judgment. This injunction holds till the Day of Judgment. But what does it mean to be superior above the Jews? Our finite minds can only interpret, because the Quran and the Hadith do not specify. However, ponder over an important reality. If one had claimed over 2000 years ago that Christians would have a superior position over the Jews, people would have scoffed at the notion. After all, the followers of Prophet Jesus came from the lower class and were the disenfranchised community. Even more, it is believed that the Christians numbered no more than 150 to 200 followers when Prophet Jesus was lifted into heaven. Yet, God promised Prophet Jesus that his followers would be superior and above the Jews. Such is the will of God and He is the one and only sovereign God who can give honor to anyone He desires and withhold it from anyone. Recall that God honored the Sons of Jacob who became the chosen people over others. But after sending thousands of prophets over a span of 2000 years, God took away their honor and status after their rebellion and numerous transgressions. The culmination of their perfidy was when they "crucified" their Messiah. The irony is that God made the followers of Prophet Jesus superior and above the Jews as a punishment until the Day of Judgment. One can ask: in what ways are the Christians superior to the Jews?

In my humble assessment, there are two aspects that establish superiority. First, in terms of faith, the Christians are more devoted and believe in God more than the Jews. Christians in comparison to the Jews believe in God and attend church. Among the nearly six million Jews that live in Israel, more than one fourth is atheist, according to a study conducted by Andrew Greeley of the University of Chicago. One out of five belongs to Orthodox sects who live according to the Torah and Talmud. Second, the Christians are superior in the success of spreading their belief system. As previously mentioned, the followers of Prophet Jesus at the time of his ascension were in the hundreds while the Jews numbered in the hundreds of thousands. Two thousand years later, Christianity, despite being an offshoot of Judaism, had nearly two billion followers as opposed to less than 15 million Jews worldwide. There was the prolific spread of Christianity over the millennia whereas the Jews were stateless up until 1948. In fact, it was through Christian support from the West that led to the formation of the state of Israel. Hence, the promise made to Prophet Jesus has been and continues to be fulfilled. It is also worthwhile to mention that verse 55 does not say that Muslims are superior to the Jews. Rather, Christian supremacy over Jews is emphasized because of Jewish rejection and crucifixion of Prophet Jesus. The last part of the verse is the statement **"Then you all will return to Me, and I will judge among you in matters on which you disagree."** It is on the Day of Judgment that all truth will be known and God will judge among the people. Verse 55 should not be viewed as a categorical denunciation of all Jewish people. After all, God did send more prophets to them than any other community. People do not have any right to judge the Jewish people and carry out acts of hate. It is troubling to see the spread of anti-Jewish rhetoric worldwide, including the Muslim world. Anti-Jewish sentiments are on the rise in places like Russia, Germany, Argentina, Morocco, Lebanon, etc. Muslims in particular are called to fairness and justice without allowing prejudices to dictate personal actions. In Surah 5:8 it states, **"Believers, be upstanding for God as witnesses for justice; and do not let the hatred of some people hurt you so much that you are not fair. Be fair; that is kin to conscience. And be conscious of God, for God is aware of what you do."** And this is further supported by Surah 4:135: **"Believers, be supporters of justice, as witnesses to God, even be it against yourselves, or your parents or relatives; whether one be rich or poor, God is closer and more worthy than either. And do not follow desire, lest you swerve from justice; and if you pervert it or neglect it, God is aware of what you do."** Thus let God be the judge and the servant be the servant.

In verse 56 we read about those people who reject faith and its consequences. It states, **"And as for those who scoff, I will punish them with severe punishment in the world and the hereafter, and they will have no saviors."** Although this verse may seem strict to some, the reality is that God

Chapter 5: Aal-E-Imran (The Family of Imran)

outlines the criteria of right and wrong and establishes reward structures and associated punishments for actions. Those who reject faith and commit unlawful acts must be held accountable, and without it, true justice cannot be established. In verse 56 we read about his punishment but in verse 57 we read about His generosity. God states, **"And as for those who believe and do good works, God will pay them their rewards. And God does not love wrongdoers."** God displays His love and generosity by rewarding those who have faith and perform good deeds. One important theme that resonates throughout the Quran is that when God mentions punishments the next verse invariably is accompanied by statements that reinforce His mercy and compassion.

God states in verse 58, **"That is what We tell you of the signs and the wise admonition."** Again, God reminds the Muslims and the delegation from Najran that these utterances from Prophet Muhammad are indeed the truth and full of wisdom. The Christian delegation that came to Medina was present as these verses were being revealed. They were surprised to hear such details regarding Prophet Jesus' miracles and his teachings. The Christian delegates knew that Prophet Muhammad being an Arab did not possess the knowledge of the scriptures, and this was revealing information that they did not know. Ultimately, the Christian delegates left Medina satisfied and vowed to pay taxes and keep the peace. The delegates having spent approximately ten days in the company of the Prophet and hearing the Quran from him were moved by the whole experience. In my opinion, open minded Christians today would also accept the universality of the Quran in a similar fashion if they only were introduced to its essential teachings. Because the Bible has been interpreted in a variety of ways, Christianity is divided into numerous denominations that strongly disagree even on the basics. Muslims, on the other hand, speak with a single voice on what the Quran teaches. There has been no new progression of knowledge or councils convened that have fundamentally altered basic Islamic doctrines. The core Islamic beliefs have been preserved for over 1400 years.

By contrast, Christian doctrine has evolved over the centuries from the time of the Apostles to this day. Some core disagreements on the Christian creed are as follows. The first instance in which Christians were divided was during the Apostles' time when Paul disputed with the twelve Apostles of Prophet Jesus on preaching to the Gentiles and adherence to the Jewish Law. Another example was the dispute among the early Christians on the identity of Jesus Christ. Was he man or God? Did he appear on earth in human form or was he pure spirit? Regarding the Bible, what books and letters should be included in the Bible? Interestingly, the accepted books of the Old Testament vary among Catholics and Protestants. The Catholic Church recognizes seven divine books called the Apocrypha that are not included in the Protestant Bible. Christians disagree with the sacrament of the Holy Communion. Catholic and Orthodox churches believe that the bread and wine contain the true presence of the body of Jesus whereas the Protestants claim that the bread and wine are a symbolic representation of Jesus Christ. One final example that crystallizes the evolution and development of Christian doctrine pertains to the Rapture. The outlandish claims include believers will vanish while others are left behind, the dead will be raised up, and doomsday nightmares of the end times. Today's Protestant and Evangelical beliefs are so unbelievable that Luther, Calvin, John Wesley, and virtually all Popes would surely reject their conceptualizations.

These are but some eclectic examples of divergent positions but the most significant distortion occurs when Christians claim that Prophet Jesus is the son of God as a result of his miraculous birth and miracles. In verse 59, God reminds both Christians and Muslims that the creation of Prophet Jesus by His command is the same as the creation of Prophet Adam. The verse is, **"Jesus was to God like Adam was: God created him from dust, then said, 'Be,' and he was."** Surely no Christian claims that Prophet Adam is somehow divine, because he had neither a father nor a mother. How then can Christians believe that Prophet Jesus was the son of God? This is a belief that emerged long after Prophet Jesus' ascension to heaven and was later disputed centuries after. However, Muslims steadfastly believe that Prophet Jesus was a servant of God born by His command, and he neither died and nor was he crucified. Christians and Muslims do agree that he was lifted into heaven and will return in the same manner. In light of this last verse, one can appreciate the notion of Prophet Jesus being the second Adam. Prophet Jesus can only be considered the second Adam by the method by which he was created. God uttered **"Be"** and both Prophets Adam and Jesus came to be.

The commentary of Surah 3:84 and Surah 42:13 is very similar to that of 2:136. Both of those appear below:

> **Say "We believe in God, and in what has been revealed to us, and in what was revealed to Abraham, Ishmael, Isaac, Jacob, and the Tribes; and in what was given to Moses, Jesus, and the prophets, from their Lord. We do not discriminate between individuals among them; for we submit to God."** (Surah 3:84)

Chapter 5: Aal-E-Imran (The Family of Imran)

"God has prescribed for you what God enjoined on Noah, by which We inspired you, and what We enjoined Abraham, Moses, and Jesus, that you be steadfast in faith and not be disunited in it. What you call them to is too much for idolaters. God chooses for God whomever God wants, and guides to the divine whoever turns to God." (Surah 42:13)

6

An-Nisa

(The Women)

Surah 4 is entitled "An-Nisa" which means "the women" and articulates the rights of women. During pre-Islamic Arabia, women were the true disenfranchised community and had virtually no rights. In fact, this was a time when infant girls would be buried alive due to the Arab preference for boys. They of course could not work, vote, inherit property, freely marry and divorce their husbands, and had no religious and social protection of any kind. Western observers may be shocked to know that Islam came to correct this imbalance and guaranteed equal rights for women. In fact, the Quran is the only religious text that has a chapter devoted to the rights of women. To reiterate, this is unique to the Quran and a book or chapter devoted to women is to be found in no other religious tradition. Also, the Bible blamed women for original sin which contributed historically to horrific iniquities against women. Islam not only rejects original sin but the Quran specifically blames Adam for the transgression in heaven. Ultimately, the Quran states in Surah seven that God forgave both Adam and Eve.

Surah Nisa was revealed in Medina between 625 and 628. As mentioned repeatedly, the Quran was revealed to Prophet Muhammad in a piecemeal fashion as evolving circumstances required. A good illustration of this is the rights and status of women in Islamic society. There was no mention in the Quran of individual rights in the first thirteen years of Prophet Muhammad's preaching to the Arabs in Mecca. The reason was because Muslims were not allowed to practice their religion freely or even express their Islamic affiliation. If God at the time had revealed rights of inheritance, marriage, dowry, divorce, etc. without the necessary means of implementation, then what purpose would such passages serve? The Muslims were a tiny community of less than a few hundred who were struggling just to worship the One True God. However, this changed when the people of

Chapter 6: An-Nisa (The Women)

Medina invited Prophet Muhammad to worship freely and establish a Muslim society. During this time in Medina, God sent numerous revelations that would govern all aspects of Muslim life. Hence, all injunctions and prohibitions that encompass the totality of a Muslim's life trace back to the Medina period. Such is the case with the rights of women discussed in Surah Nisa. Again, let me parenthetically mention that Islam gave women the right to inherit property, earn a living, vote, divorce their husbands, and numerous other rights that did not exist in the "civilized" western world up until quite recently. In fact, I am ashamed to say as an American that it was only in the early twentieth century that we allowed women to divorce their husbands independent of the charge of adultery, desertion, or alcoholism. It was only in the mid-twentieth century that we allowed divorce on the basis of incompatibility (Friedman). Moreover, women were viewed by 19th century thinkers to have limited intellect because pregnancy and delivery of children would shrink their brains. The German philosopher Arthur Schopenhauer held similar contentions. In his essay *On Women*, he writes, "Women are directly adapted to act as the nurses and educators of our early childhood, for the simple reason that they themselves are childish, foolish, and short-sighted—in a word, are big children all their lives." However, Muslim women were judges and scholars since the seventh century. Islam was even prescient in the area of contraception use to aid in family planning, which Christians continue to struggle with today.

With this as a preamble on Surah Nisa, let us return to our topic of examining Quranic verses on Prophet Jesus. Beginning with verse 150, God delineates the sins of the Jewish people. Among the sins specified is their accusation against Lady Mary and the crucifixion of Prophet Jesus. In Verses 156-159 God states, **"On account of their scoffing, too, and their monstrous slander of Mary, and on account of their saying, 'We killed the Messiah Jesus, Son of Mary, messenger of God, whereas they did not kill him, they did not crucify him, although it was made to seem thus to them. As for those who differ on this, they are certainly in doubt about it. They have no knowledge about it, only following conjecture; but they surely did not kill him: rather God raised him up to the divine presence; and God is almighty, most wise. And none of the people of scripture will fail to believe in him before his death; and on the day of resurrection he will be a witness against them."**

In Verse 156, we learn that the Jews denied Prophet Jesus and rejected faith. The Jews knew that Prophet Jesus was a true prophet of God, but they nevertheless rejected him because he undermined the authority of the Sanhedrin clergy. They not only denied Prophet Jesus and conspired to kill him but accused his mother of committing an immoral act. John 8:41 says "Then they said to him, 'We were not born of fornication.'" Any upright human being would find such an accusation offensive, but to utter this type of falsehood against a prophet of God is quite reprehensible. Moreover, the Quran identifies that this false charge was more so against his righteous and God-fearing mother than Prophet Jesus himself. Islam and Muslims have the highest regard for Lady Mary and accord her the utmost love and deference she rightly deserves. Muslims believe Lady Mary devoted her entire life worshiping God in the Holy Temple and that Prophet Jesus' birth was the result of the command of the Almighty God.

In Verse 157, God addressed another false indictment that the Jews leveled, namely that they had crucified Prophet Jesus. The Jews for centuries claimed that they had crucified Prophet Jesus, and because of it, the Christians persecuted the Jews throughout Christian history. The Gospels clearly identify the Jews as responsible for the crucifixion of Christ. Indeed, the New Testament contains the statements of Prophet Jesus and his disciples directly blaming the Jews for this horrific act. Here are some passages from the Gospels. John 8:37 "I know that you are Abraham's descendants; yet you seek to kill me, because my words have no place in you." John 11:48 and 11:53 state, "If we let Him go on like this, all men will believe in Him, and the Romans will come and take away both our place and our nation." ... "So from that day on they planned together to kill Him." Luke 23:20 and onward state, "Pilate, wanting to release Jesus, addressed them again, but they kept on calling out, saying, 'Crucify! Crucify Him!' And he said to them the third time, 'Why, what evil has this man done? I have found in Him no guilt demanding death; therefore I will punish Him and release Him. But they were insistent, with loud voices asking that He be crucified. And their voices began to prevail. And Pilate pronounced sentence that their demand be granted." Luke 24:20 "How the chief priest and our rulers delivered Him up to the sentence of death and crucified Him." These are only a handful of passages that place the responsibility of Christ's crucifixion at the hands of the Jewish authority. For nearly 2000 years the Christians did not waiver in this regard. This did change in the Catholic Church when Vatican II convened. In the early 1960s the Catholic Church convened its 21st Ecumenical council to review, revise, and update various positions of the Catholic doctrine. As a result of this council the Catholic position absolved the Jews of the crucifixion of Christ. Instead, it blamed all of humanity beginning with Adam to the last human to come for his crucifixion. This may be acceptable today due to this revision of church

Chapter 6: An-Nisa (The Women)

doctrine, but it contradicts the verbatim statements of Prophet Jesus and his Apostles. Muslims however are quite strict with their holy texts. Therefore, in accordance with the Quran and Hadith, all Muslims believe that Prophet Jesus was not crucified but was lifted up into heaven. When God had decided that the Jews as a whole rejected faith and were planning to kill Prophet Jesus, God sent Angel Gabriel to inform Prophet Jesus of the conspiracy and that he would be lifted up into heaven. When the Roman soldiers came to arrest Prophet Jesus God had already raised him. Taking his place was a man with the same appearance as Prophet Jesus, and he was arrested instead.

We will discuss in detail in later chapters incontrovertible and overwhelming Biblical passages that establish that Prophet Jesus was not harmed or crucified. Therefore, I would urge the reader to consider the evidence and arguments presented in the final chapter. However, let us briefly share a few passages that support the Muslim claim. First, we read in Psalms 20:6 which states, "Now I know that the Lord saves his anointed; He will answer him for His holy heaven with the saving strength of His right hand." This verse says that God will save "His anointed" with the strength of his right hand. But who is His anointed and who is His right hand? No one has a greater claim to be the anointed one except Jesus Christ because Christ literally means "the anointed one." Can this verse be any clearer that God will save Jesus Christ and he will do so "with the strength of His right hand?" If it does not, then consider two similar passages. Psalms 28:8 says, "He is a saving defense to His anointed." And Psalms 41:1-2 states, "And the Lord will deliver him in a day of trouble the Lord will protect him and keep him alive. And he shall be called blessed upon the Earth. And do not give him over to the desires of his enemies." These two passages, especially the latter, can only refer to Prophet Jesus because they are very explicit that God will save and protect the anointed one.

Such passages confirm the Muslim position that Prophet Jesus did not perish or die on the cross but was saved by Almighty God. The question is how was he saved and who is the Right Hand of God that saved him? Through inductive analysis we can assert without equivocation that the phrase "the strength of His right hand" can only refer to Angel Gabriel. As has been mentioned previously, the word Gabriel in Hebrew literally means "strength of God." Muslims believe that Angel Gabriel has the highest position and status among the angels and he is nearest to God. In fact, in Luke 1:19 it is confirmed that Angel Gabriel is very close to God and prepared to do God's will. This verse in Luke is as follows, "The Angel answered and said to him, I am Gabriel, who stands in the presence of God." Hence, it was Angel Gabriel who raised Prophet Jesus before he was harmed, and this position can be sustained by the Biblical passages above. **"Rather, God raised him up to the divine presence; and God is almighty, most wise."**

Given that we have just established that Prophet Jesus was not crucified, how then can the Jews be blamed? The answer is that the Jews had murdered prophets in the past and they did so knowing that they were killing messengers of God. When Prophet Jesus came to them performing miracles, they acknowledge that he was the Christ. In John 3:1-2 we read, "Now there was a man of the Pharisees, named Nicodemus, a ruler of the Jews." This man came to him by night and said to him, 'Rabbi we know that you have come from God as a teacher for no one can do these signs that you do unless God is with him.'" John 9:22 says, "For the Jews had already agreed that if anyone confessed Him to be Christ, he was to be put out of the synagogue." Therefore, when the Jews realized that he was a threat to their authority and denounced their hypocritical ways, the Jews became angry and plotted to kill Prophet Jesus. They brought him to the Roman authority and charged him with treason. And throughout the process the Jews were convinced that they had arrested and successfully crucified Prophet Jesus. Actions are predicated on intentions. They intended and plotted to kill him, and from their myopic vantage point, this is what they had successfully done. The act of saving him occurred through divine intervention, but humans are held accountable for what they do on earth. In a similar vein, should idol worshipers not be accountable for worshiping statues whom they consider to be god? Even though they are not worshiping the true God, this act of idolatry is nevertheless considered a sin by God. Consequently, those who participated in the crucifixion of Christ will be accountable on the Day of Judgment. In verse 159, it is said, **"And none of the people of scripture will fail to believe in him before his death; and on the day of resurrection he will be a witness against them."**

Thus far we have covered the sins of the Jewish people as they pertain to Prophet Jesus. The next few passages that will be examined address the Christian belief that Prophet Jesus was divine and part of the triune Godhead. Although an entire chapter is devoted to the trinity doctrine, let me briefly mention that the Muslim position is that this belief is a terrible attack on, as well as an obvious misrepresentation of, the One true God. It clearly goes against the first commandment and defies logic and reason. This is the single most important source of division not only between Muslims and Christians but also Christians and Jews. The belief that Prophet Jesus was simultaneously God and the son of

Chapter 6: An-Nisa (The Women)

God is simply unacceptable and Muslims are of the conviction that this type of a transgression comes very close to idolatry. Hinduism for instance has many gods that evidently took human as well as animal forms, and these gods lived among the creatures of the earth. When these "gods" died people began to create their images in idol form. Christians would surely join Muslims and Jews to denounce these Hindu gods. Likewise, Muslims reject that an obedient servant of God would ever profess that others should worship him as part of the triune Godhead. The Quran is explicit in denouncing this extreme doctrine. In verses 171-172 God states: **"People of scripture, do not go to excess in your religion, and do not say anything about God but the truth. The Messiah Jesus Son of Mary was only a messenger, a word, from God, which God sent down to Mary, a spirit from God. So believe in God and God's messengers. And do not speak of a trinity; it is best for you to refrain. God is one sole divinity, too transcendent to have a son, in possession of all in the heavens and on earth. And God is a good enough patron. The Messiah is not too proud to be a servant of God, nor are the intimate angels. Any too proud to serve God, being self-aggrandizing, God will gather in, all."**

These two verses address the extreme viewpoint that Christians have regarding the trinity. In verses 171 and 172 God reminds us who Jesus Christ really was (messenger of God) and reaffirms his miraculous creation. Since these issues have been thoroughly discussed in earlier sections, a few remarks on Prophet Jesus being a **"spirit from God."** are warranted. First and foremost, this does not convey any sort of divine nature that was transmitted to Prophet Jesus. This can be asserted without equivocation because the entire verse denounces the Christian belief that Prophet Jesus is somehow divine. Secondly, the Muslim position in this phrase is referring to the creation of Prophet Jesus. Every human being from the beginning of creation and until today is comprised of two basic elements: the physical body and the spirit. The spirit/soul gives the physical body life. For example, in the creation of Prophet Adam God first created him from clay and then breathed the spirit into him which gave Adam life. Therefore, the spirit is the source of all human life and it has been created by God and proceeds from Him. Muslims believe that although the joining of an egg and sperm produces the material needed for the physical flesh it is the spirit that gives life to the embryonic child. The Hadiths make it very clear that God commands his angels to breathe the spirit into the fetus during the fourth month of the pregnancy. Sahih Bukhari, Volume 4, Book 55, Number 549 mentions, "As regards to your creation, every one of you is collected in the womb of his mother for the first forty days, and then he becomes a clot for another forty days, and then a piece of flesh for another forty days. Then God sends an angel to write four words: He writes his deeds, time of his death, means of his livelihood, and whether he will be wretched or blessed (in religion). Then the soul is breathed into his body." This is the manner by which all human beings come into this world. This process is referred to as ensoulment. Christianity throughout the ages has failed to identify exactly when the soul is joined to the physical flesh. This is why many Christians suggest that life begins at the point of conception. By contrast, other Christians are in doubt as to when this occurs. Parenthetically, St. Augustine in his commentary of the Bible postulated that ensoulment occurs during the third month of pregnancy. However, in the case of Prophet Jesus we know that he was created by the command of God (**"Be!"**) which he bestowed onto Lady Mary. At the appropriate time, by the command of God, Angel Gabriel blew the spirit of Prophet Jesus into Lady Mary's womb. Hence, Prophet Jesus was created by a word and spirit proceeding from God. Similarly, as a result of God blowing His spirit into Prophet Adam we would not say that Prophet Adam shares in His divinity. Surah 15:29 states (for Adam), **"Now when I have put him in order and breathed some of My spirit into him, then bow down to him."**

In verse 171 God speaks against the trinity and advises Christians not to believe in it. **"So believe in God and God's messengers. And do not speak of a trinity; it is best for you to refrain."** This verse makes it very clear that Muslims worship the one true God and reject the Christian belief that Prophet Jesus is the son of God and part of the triune Godhead. God gives two simple reasons for why Prophet Jesus does not share in His divinity. First, God is one sovereign entity and is independent of anyone and anything. The phrase at the end of the verse **"God is one sole divinity,"** refers to the fact that God is far removed from all imperfections. The suggestion that God begot a son is considered to be insulting because it debases God to performing activities relegated to His creatures. Is God not powerful enough to create Jesus Christ without parent(s) as He did with Adam? God is **"Too transcendent to have a son, in possession of all in the heavens and on earth,"** The second obvious reason that God reveals for why Prophet Jesus does not share in His divinity is because Prophet Jesus worshiped God. This fact cannot be emphasized enough. In verse 172 we read that Prophet Jesus did not disdain from worshipping his Lord. Verse 172 says, **"The Messiah is not too proud to be a servant of God, nor are the intimate angels. Any too proud to serve God, being self-aggrandizing, God will gather in, all."** The Quran contains no details about his worship. However, the Gospels are replete with passages that describe his worship to God. The following are but a few passages from Luke. In Luke 5:16 as well as in 6:12 we know that he prayed to

Chapter 6: An-Nisa (The Women)

God. (5:16 "But He himself would often slip away to the wilderness and pray." Luke 6:12, "And it was at this time He went off to the mountain to pray and He spent the whole night in prayer to God.") Luke 9:18, "And it came about that while he was praying alone." Luke 11:1, "And it came about while He was praying at a certain place." Luke 22:41, "He withdrew from them about a stone's throw, knelt down and prayed." Luke 22:44, "And being in anguish, he prayed more earnestly, and his sweat was like drops of blood falling to the ground.") These verses demonstrate that Prophet Jesus worshipped God like all other servants and prophets. For Christians to claim that Prophet Jesus was divine contradicts not only those passages that establish his worship but also many others that refer to him as a man. Moreover, the contradiction is even more obvious when you stop to ponder, "How can God worship God"? This is a pagan concept of Greek and Roman mythology, which Islam rejects.

One final point on verse 172 concerns the fact that God mentions Prophet Jesus' worship of Him along with the angels. This is worth mentioning because Muslims believe that not only are the Christians guilty of making Prophet Jesus divine, but they have also extended divinity to the Holy Spirit. As the reader must be aware by now, Muslims believe that the Holy Spirit is Angel Gabriel while Christians have turned him into the third part of the Triune Godhead. The Quran teaches that angels are created beings that are completely subservient to God. Surah 21:19-20 states, **"For everyone in the skies and on earth belongs to God; even those in the presence of God are not too proud for the service of God, and neither do they weary; they celebrate the glory of God night and day, never weakening."** In fact, the Holy Spirit that Christians worship is Angel Gabriel. To establish this, let us first look at the role of the Holy Spirit as understood by Christian theologians. One important responsibility of the Holy Spirit is to guide the people to the truth. The Holy Spirit enabled the Apostles to write the inspired revelation that would over time become the Gospels and the New Testament. This is also true of the prophets of the Old Testament who received revelation and guidance from the Holy Spirit which they delivered to the people. This is further supported by Zacharias 7:12, which states, "The words which the Lord of hosts had sent by *His Spirit* through the former prophets." Muslims believe that the delivery of divine revelation is done by Angel Gabriel. We see this time and again in both the Old as well as the New Testament. Phrases like "the Angel of the Lord said" or "the Angel of the Lord appeared" is in reference to Angel Gabriel. In Genesis 16:11 the Angel of the Lord speaks to Hagar saying, "Behold you are with child, and you will bear a son; and you shall call his name Ishmael, because the Lord has given heed to you affliction." The

Christ Jesus, The Son of Mary: A Muslim Perspective

New Testament Gospels also contain Angel Gabriel delivering messages to Prophet Zachariah (Luke 1:19), Lady Mary (Luke 1:26), and Prophet Jesus (Luke 22:43).

These passages confirm that communication from God is delivered to the prophets by Angel Gabriel. But the most revealing passage that confirms the Muslim position that the Holy Spirit is Angel Gabriel is found in Revelation 1:1. It states, "The Revelation of Jesus Christ, which God gave Him to show to His bond-servants, the things which must soon take place; and He sent and communicated it by His angel." However, Christians would certainly disagree that the Holy Spirit is not Angel Gabriel but God Himself in a different form. They would go on to say that the Holy Spirit is the third person, co-eternal, and co-equal with the triune Godhead. The dilemma for Christians is that the existence and knowledge of the Holy Spirit was revealed in the last days of Prophet Jesus. In Acts 8:14-16, John the Baptist, as well as some of his apostles did not know about the Holy Spirit. These passages are as follows: "Now when the apostles in Jerusalem heard that Samaria had received the word of God, they sent them Peter and John, who came down and prayed for them that they might receive the Holy Spirit. For He had not fallen upon any of them; they had simply been baptized in the name of the Lord Jesus." Furthermore, the idea that the Holy Spirit was God was not embraced until after Prophet Jesus was lifted into heaven. It was the second ecumenical council which met in Constantinople that officially decreed the Holy Spirit as a third part of the triune Godhead. Prior to this council, there is nowhere in the New Testament that identifies the Holy Spirit as being divine or the third part of a triune God. If one acknowledges that the Holy Spirit is part of God, then why is its existence unknown to the prophets? Neither Muslims nor the Jews altered the oneness of God in this manner, and no prophet since Adam, Noah, Abraham, Moses, David, Jesus, or Muhammad has taught and worshipped anyone but the one true God. The commentary for Surah 4:163 can be interpreted similarly to Surah 6, as it invokes a list of prophets, including Prophet Jesus. Surah 4:163 states,

> "We have inspired you, as We inspired Noah and the prophets after him; We inspired Abraham, and Ishmael, and Isaac, and Jacob, and the Tribes, and Jesus, and Job, and Jonah, and Aaron, and Solomon; and We gave David thePsalms."

Chapter 8: Al-An'am (The Cattle)

7

Al-Ma'idah

(The tablecloth with food)

This Surah was named Al-Ma'idah which means "The tablecloth with food" because the disciples of Prophet Jesus requested a sign from God (see verse 111). In antiquity and even in some tribal societies today, people gather together for meals on a table cloth. This Surah was revealed during the period 629-632 CE. However, the verses that discussed Prophet Jesus were revealed in the latter months of the year 628 CE shortly after the signing of the treaty of Hudaybiya. This treaty was between Muslims who had recently migrated from Mecca to Medina and the Arab idolaters. Among the principles of the treaty was the establishment of a truce between both parties for ten years. Each side agreed not to wage war against the other in order that peaceful attempts at reconciliation could be attempted. More importantly, it allowed the Muslims who had been restricted to Medina to freely practice and preach Islam throughout the Arab peninsula. Unfortunately the terms of the treaty were severed due to an attack by an Arab pagan tribe that led to the death of some Muslims who were allied with Prophet Muhammad.

Nevertheless, during the two year period there was a dramatic increase of people embracing Islam. Muslim scholars have estimated that prior to the treaty of Hudaybiya there were approximately 2,500 to 3,000 Muslims living primarily in Medina. In-between the two years, however, the Muslim population soared to 50 to 60,000 people living throughout the Arab Peninsula. This rapid Muslim conversion demonstrates the truthfulness of Prophet Muhammad and the transformative quality of his Message. Both Arab and non-Arabs were able to witness the great change that Muslims brought to a once ignorant and lawless society and the establishment of a highly sophisticated and moral social order after Islam. A mark of a true Prophet is when they produce righteous people.

Chapter 7: Al-Ma'idah (The tablecloth with food)

The ultimate mission of a prophet is to rescue people from their own darkness and bring them to light.

> "People of scripture, Our messenger has come to you, clarifying for you much from scripture that you used to hide; and passing over a lot. Light from God has come to you, a clear Book, by which God guides those who follow divine will in ways of peace, and brings them from darkness to light, by divine leave, and guides them to a straight path."
> (Surah 5:15-16)

As discussed earlier, Muslims believe that Christians falsely associate Prophet Jesus as being God.

> "Those who say 'God is the Messiah Son of Mary' have blasphemed. Say, 'Then who can keep anything from God if God wants to annihilate the Messiah Son of Mary, his mother, and everyone on earth? It is God who has the power over the heavens and the earth and what is between them. God creates whatever God will; and God is able to do all things." (Surah 5:17)

In the above verse, God addresses the fatuous claim of Christians who believe Jesus Christ was God in the flesh. The monotheistic Abrahamic traditions would unanimously agree that the greatest offense that anyone can commit is to deny the oneness of God and associate others with the one true God. To become Muslims, we must first affirm that there is no one worthy of worship except the one supreme God. Concurrently, in the Jewish faith the first commandment is the testimony in the oneness of God and the prohibition that no one can be associated with Him. Christians also claim to believe in one God but they violate this core belief when they declare that Christ is God. The Quran calls this blasphemy. The Quran is perhaps one of the most inclusive sacred texts that speaks of religious tolerance and the protection of other religions. This is why the Quran has preserved the stories of other prophets and their universal call to worship God. However, the Quran is unusually harsh when it comes to egregious violations of the first commandment. The suggestion that the shadow of the Holy Spirit over Mary somehow produced the son of God who later died would be considered offensive to the glory and majesty of Almighty God. Furthermore, the suggestion on the part of Catholics that this resulted in a spousal relationship between the

Holy Spirit and Mary would be just as reprehensible, and has no scriptural grounding.

Verse 17 ends by asking a rhetorical question about the temporal existence of Jesus and Mary. Trying to appeal to our intellect, the Quran forces us to ponder that God is capable of destroying His creation without any challenger to stop Him. One of God's attributes is that God is all powerful. As such, if God intended to destroy Jesus Christ, Lady Mary and everyone on earth, can anyone challenge His authority and will? If Jesus Christ was God, does he possess the power to prevent God from destroying him and his mother? According to the Gospels, in the Garden of Gethsemane, Jesus Christ prayed fervently for the "removal of the cup" which refers to the crucifixion, suffering and torture that was to come. In fact, he said "not by my will, but Thy will," illustrating the higher power and authority that God "the Father" possessed. Moreover, this event demonstrates the lack of knowledge that Jesus Christ had for what God the Father preordained for him. This lack of knowledge indicates his limitations, and God has no limitations. Also, God is not only all powerful but is the creator of the heavens and the earth and everything in between, including Prophet Jesus. Although Prophet Jesus was created through Immaculate Conception (born to a virgin), he still owes his existence to the One God who created him. By nature, an Almighty God must be self-sustaining and cannot be created.

> **"Those who say God is the Messiah Son of Mary have certainly blasphemed: whereas the Messiah said, 'Children of Israel, worship God, my Lord and your Lord.' For whoever associates anyone with God, God has forbidden the garden; his place is the fire. And there is no savior for those who do wrong."** (Surah 5:72)

In the above verse, God again responds to the Christian claim that Christ is God. The Quran states that Jesus Christ never professed his divinity and in fact declared to the Children of Israel the importance of worshiping "...my Lord and your Lord." We read throughout the Gospels that Prophet Jesus acknowledged the oneness of God and the need to worship Him alone. In John 20:17 Jesus said, "Stop clinging to me, for I have not yet ascended to the Father; but go to my brethren and say to them, 'I ascend to my Father and your Father, and my God and your God.'" In Mark 12:29 Jesus states: "The foremost is, 'Hear O Israel! The Lord our God is one Lord.'" These passages clearly illustrate Prophet Jesus' acknowledgement of a higher power whom he worshipped. More importantly, as has been mentioned several times, there is not a single verse throughout the Gospels where Jesus Christ asked his followers to worship him.

The latter part of verse 72 is **"For whoever associates anyone with God, God has forbidden the garden; his place is the fire. And there is no savior for those who do wrong."** Although such a statement does not appear in the Gospels, it nevertheless comports to the teachings of any true prophet of God. In Matthew 19:17 Jesus says, "Why are you asking me about what is good? There is only One who is good; but if you wish to enter into life, keep the commandments." This passage categorically declares that following the commandments enables the servant to achieve the highest goal of paradise, and of course the first commandment is the belief and worship of one God. Any violation of this basic creed goes against the Abrahamic covenant. For such violators, there is no heavenly reward. Muslims believe those Christians that proclaim that Jesus Christ is God are contradicting Prophet Jesus who told his followers to worship one God and adhere to the commandments. If this were not enough, Christians go one step further by making the one God into three deities.

> **"Those who say God is one third of a trinity have certainly blasphemed, for there is no deity but one God. So if they do not stop what they are saying, a painful penalty will strike those of them who blaspheme."** (Surah 5:73)

The Quran calls this understanding of the Divine as an abomination. The "Father" is the entity whom Muslims worship. But the point of departure comes when Christians claim the deification of the Son and the Holy Spirit. The Holy Spirit is hardly mentioned in the Scriptures and nowhere in the Gospel has it been referred to as being divine. The acknowledgement and worship of one God has been a tradition that has been practiced from the time of Adam to Noah, Abraham and his sons, Moses, and David, and including Jesus Christ and Prophet Muhammad. To believe Jesus Christ (a man) and the Holy Spirit (an angel) are co-equal to God is a sin against the true God who will judge with a severe punishment. However, the special quality of the Quran is that whenever God speaks of His wrath and punishment He immediately follows it with His glorious quality of mercy and forgiveness.

> **"Why don't they turn to God and seek forgiveness of God, since God is most forgiving, most merciful."** (Surah 5:74)

Christ Jesus, The Son of Mary: A Muslim Perspective

The Muslim understanding is that God created human beings in order that we may get to know and worship Him. Unlike other creation (angels, trees, mountains, animals, etc.), human beings are endowed with free will which allows them to accept or reject. If an entity has the option to refuse and commit rebellion but chooses to accept faith freely, this is much more pleasing to God. Given that humans have free will where the servant can choose to do good or commit evil, sins are inevitable. As such, repentance is required to expiate sins. In fact, the word for repentance in Arabic *Tawba* comes from the root "to return." Humans are constantly returning back to God. The Prophet Muhammad said "O God, there is no refuge from You but to You." This important idea of repentance is mentioned repeatedly in the Quran and it is not unique to Islam. Jesus Christ taught the value of repentance throughout his ministry and the call to repent for sins appears at least 50 times in the New Testament. Verse 75 speaks to our reason by humanizing Jesus Christ and Mary. The verse says:

> **"The Messiah Son of Mary was only a messenger. Messengers had already passed away before him. And his mother was a veracious woman. The two of them both used to eat food. See how We clarify the signs to them; then see how deluded they are."**

Here, the true identity of Jesus Christ is revealed, namely that he was a Prophet of God like several of those that came and passed away before him. The verse talks about the fact that Jesus Christ and Mary were humans and dependent upon basic needs. God calls our attention to the daily sustenance of food needed by both for survival, thereby demonstrating their humanity. Basic needs such as eating, drinking and sleeping are human limitations which even angels are not bound by, let alone God.

The phrase **"The two of them both used to eat food,"** needs to be mentioned. Here, God specifies two persons only (Jesus and his mother) eating together. According to the New Testament and church traditions, Lady Mary was betrothed to Joseph prior to the conception of Jesus. Such an arrangement is not corroborated by the Quran or Hadith. However, the notion that Lady Mary was married to Joseph prior to the conception of Jesus is problematic because it calls into question the virgin birth of Jesus Christ. Therefore, it is very likely that Lady Mary was not even betrothed to Joseph especially prior to the conception and after the birth of Jesus. Such an arrangement is inconsistent with Lady Mary's response to Angel Gabriel when he informed her that she will bear a child. In the Bible,

Chapter 7: Al-Ma'idah (The tablecloth with food)

she responded: "How can that be when no man has touched me"? If she indeed was betrothed to Joseph, as Christians claim, then the response should have been "when will that be"? Although Muslims and Christians unequivocally believe in the virgin and miraculous birth of Prophet Jesus, the Christian account leads to ambiguity emanating from what ultimately became of Joseph. Did Mary have children with Joseph? Did Jesus have siblings?

The Surah continues with verse 76 as follows:

"Say, 'Do you worship what has no power to harm or help you, rather than God? God is the one who hears all and knows all.'"

After identifying Prophet Jesus as a messenger of God, verse 76 asks Christians whether they would worship someone who does not have ultimate power. Through this question, God reveals the irrationality of human beings who worship false gods that are inferior and unworthy of worship. The human intellect is naturally predisposed to believe in a God without limitations. For example, there are those who worship idols of their own manufacture using dirt, wood, and stone to create their gods. The true God in reality is not created but is self-existent (meaning He had no creator), all powerful, and all knowing. These are three basic attributes of God that should be used to judge the truthfulness of any object being worshiped. Hence, idols should not be worshiped and nor should human beings because they are created, and as such, embody limitations. Christians who believe that Prophet Jesus, a human being, is God must recognize that he was created and lacked power and knowledge. We read in Matthew 24:36, "But of that day and hour no one knows, not even the angels of heaven, nor the son, but the Father alone." Prophet Jesus did not know when the Day of Judgment will come and deferred that knowledge to God. Moreover, recall in our earlier discussion the events leading up to the crucifixion in which he fervently prays to God to assuage the suffering that was to come. These passages demonstrate a lack of knowledge and power of Prophet Jesus and deference to a greater authority. Therefore, Prophet Jesus does not fulfill the criteria of one who would be classified as divine. The Quran again asks **"Do you worship what has no power to harm or help you, rather than God?"** The Quran calls this an extreme position of faith.

"Say, 'People of scripture, don't overdo your religion unrealistically, yet do not follow the desires of people who already went astray before, who misled many and strayed from the balanced way.'" (Surah 5:77)

Christ Jesus, The Son of Mary: A Muslim Perspective

In the above verse God advises Christians and Jews to remain within the parameters of their religion. Muslims believe Jews exceed the bounds by denying and disobeying God, and killing prophets whereas the Christians exceed their religion by elevating Prophet Jesus to a divine status. Both of these extreme viewpoints are egregious and not the embodiment of truth and virtue. Extremism in any form leads to misguided actions especially in matters of religion in which questioning of religious dogmas are considered wavering of an established faith. Moreover, as religious beliefs and traditions are passed on through generations, the strength and commitment to those false beliefs and practices grow stronger. Challenging such beliefs is seen as heresy and blasphemy. For example, it is the established tenet of Christianity that Jesus Christ is one of three in the triune Godhead. However, the divinity of Jesus Christ was disputed among Christians for four centuries. In 325 A.D. a council convened in Nicea (present day Turkey) to unify the Church's position regarding Jesus Christ's identity. Prior to this council, there had been diverse views regarding Prophet Jesus' life and who he actually was. Some Christians believe he was pure spirit and others believe he was a human being and not divine, while others believed he was divine as well as a man. Consequently, the council persuaded the majority of the Bishops to affirm the position that Prophet Jesus was Divine with a human body. This established the trinity doctrine and became the core principal of Christianity as it exists today. Furthermore, a second ecumenical council convened in Constantinople in 381 A.D. to further establish the Holy Spirit as a third component of the triune Godhead. What if these clergy were incorrect in their human assessment, as the Quran affirms? Clearly, this would not be the only documented incident. Soon after the Nicene Creed was established, a select group of clergy convinced Emperor Constantine to reverse the original Nicene position. In essence, the official Church teaching sanctioned by the Emperor that emerged was that Jesus Christ was not divine but a created human being. This new doctrine that lasted numerous centuries became widespread to an extent that a visible majority of the clergy as well as the laity at the time renounced Jesus Christ's divinity. A second example that validates the claim of the reversal of Church positions can be found in the acceptance of certain New Testament books and Epistles that were once rejected. For instance, the Gospel of John and the Book of Revelation were not always seen as divinely inspired texts. The widespread acceptance of these texts came much later and they became a part of the New Testament. This is not surprising, given that the New Testament of today differs between the Protestant, Catholic, and Orthodox churches. Finally, for more than a thousand years, the Catholic Church allowed the Pope and the clergy to be married and procreate. In fact, some Popes actually kept concubines. However,

Chapter 7: Al-Ma'idah (The tablecloth with food)

in the 11th century the Church changed its position and forbade marriage for all clergy in order to protect their wealth and avoid corruption. At that time, examples of nepotism and cases of inheritance improperly distributed plagued the Church. There are numerous other examples of the Church adopting opposite positions of its predecessors. When these decisions were being made, the public was in the dark, both literally as well as figuratively. Most people did not know how to read and did not have access to the texts as possessing a Bible was once forbidden. Indeed, the statement of the Quran **"Do not follow the desires of people who already went astray before, who misled many and strayed from the balanced way,"** makes appropriate sense when viewed from this perspective.

Given the information revolution of today, the onus of responsibility is on the individual to seek the truth by tapping into the various texts that are available to the aspirant. It is important to inculcate a desire within oneself to seek the truth even if it goes against one's core belief system or the established order. The example of Galileo highlights in a vivid way an individual's search for the truth. During Galileo's time, the geocentric version of the universe was the dominant paradigm that was taught by the Church. The Bible was used to perpetuate this interpretation (in particular Genesis Chapter 1, verses 1-19). As a scientist, through observation and testing, Galileo correctly theorized that the sun does not rotate around the earth but the obverse. This well-established fact that is known by our elementary students today was viewed as heresy and led to Galileo's house arrest. More than three centuries elapsed for the Church to issue an exculpatory edict, thereby vindicating Galileo.

It is now evident that the Church misinterpreted these important matters. Likewise, Muslims believe that the notion of the trinity is an exaggeration in religion and must be reexamined. Through this reexamination, Christians too may begin to recognize that the trinity is shrouded in ambiguity and contradiction.

Another great example of the development of dogma, with very little biblical support and promoted by individuals, is today's Evangelical Protestant's view of the Rapture. John Nelson Darby, a minister of the Church of Ireland - a branch of the Anglican Church- in the 19th century, promoted his belief of dispensational premillennialism. This idea is the belief that Jesus will raise his believers before a seven-year period of Tribulation, and then proceed to reign on Earth for 1,000 years. Cyrus Scofield disseminated this belief through the promotion of the *Scofield Reference Bible*, which he annotated and edited in 1909. Darby's version of the Rapture is the basis of Evangelical Christian's obsession;

which is new in Christian eschatology – or the study of the Last Days. For more than eighteen hundred years none of the apostles, popes, or saints had written about, believed, or spoken about the Rapture in this manner. In fact, not even Martin Luther or John Calvin – the principle founders of the Protestant Reformation – shared these views. Therefore, how then can Darby's viewpoint on The Rapture be legitimate as well as credible? However, there are millions upon millions of Christians that obsess about this belief of the Rapture. After all, individuals will be held accountable on the Day of Judgment for their faith as well as their actions. Following the teachings of one's forefathers or ignorance will be feeble excuses on the Day of Resurrection. Muslims believe that even prior to individual reckoning; God will first direct His line of questioning towards prophets who were the primary carriers of the message. The Quran states:

> **"One day God will gather the messengers and say, 'What was the response that you were given?' They will say, 'We have no knowledge; it is You who know all hidden secrets."** (Surah 5:109)

I would like to highlight two important points that pertain to this verse. First, in Islam, God takes the responsibility of revealing Himself to the Children of Adam in order that they may serve and worship Him alone. This is fulfilled by sending prophets and revelation to the various nations and communities in order that they may be guided. As such, it is on this basis that humans become accountable for their faith and actions, and they will be elevated or debased thereby. However, prior to individual accountability will be the questioning of prophets as to the response they received to the Divine message.

A second important point that is made in the verse is the recognition of the limited knowledge of the prophets and an acknowledgment of the total fullness and completeness of the knowledge possessed by God Almighty. Some may ask why an All-Knowing God who possesses perfect knowledge would pose a question that He has full knowledge of the answer to. This in fact is a rhetorical question to pronounce the establishment of justice so that all who are present may know of God's decree. At that time, the prophets who were the most righteous and closest to God will be humbled by His glory and majesty. The prophets will not be concerned for themselves but for the respective communities they were sent to.

Chapter 7: Al-Ma'idah (The tablecloth with food)

From verse 110 to the rest of the chapter, God addresses Jesus Christ and reveals a future dialogue that will take place on the Day of Judgment. Verse 110 states:

> **"Then God will say, 'Jesus Son of Mary, remember My favor to you and your mother when I strengthened you with the holy spirit—you spoke to the people in the cradle and in maturity—and when I taught you scripture and wisdom, the Torah and the Gospel. And you fashion the figure of a bird from clay, by My permission; then you breathe into it and it becomes a bird, by My permission. And you heal the blind and the leprous, by My permission. And I kept the Children of Israel away from you when you brought them the proofs and the scoffers said, 'This is obvious sorcery.'"**
> (Surah 5:110)

Here, God reminds Jesus Christ of the numerous favors that were bestowed upon him and that were produced exclusively by God's permission. An often overlooked favor is that God chose an extraordinarily righteous woman to be Jesus' mother. Also, God strengthened him with the Holy Spirit that protected him throughout. Finally, in this verse, God reaffirms that the miracles performed by Jesus were not his, but rather produced by God alone. Interestingly, the Book of Acts 2:22 depict the miracles performed by Jesus in a similar manner (by God's permission). The above mentioned Quranic verse narrates the explicit blessings that were given to Prophet Jesus, but the following verse expresses a blessing that was hidden from him, namely the choosing of his disciples and inspiring faith in them. Verse 111 states:

> **"And We inspired the apostles to believe in Me and My messenger. They said, 'We believe; witness that we surrender to God.'"**

Again, I find fascinating the portrayal of the disciples in the two scriptures. Whereas the Quran preserves the faith and loyalty of the disciples and followers of Jesus, the Bible depicts them as unfaithful, disloyal, and cowardly. For instance, Peter (the rock on which the Catholic Church was built upon) denied Jesus on three different occasions. Judas turned Jesus Christ to the authorities for 30 coins, and the rest of the apostles fled when Jesus was being persecuted. Conversely, Muslims reject such a depiction and honor the followers of Jesus. Indeed, the Quranic view is consistent with a passage in John's Gospel that states that the disciples were chosen by God. In John 17:6 it says, "I have manifested Your name to the men whom You gave me out of the world; they were Yours and You gave them to me, and they have kept Your word." How can God choose such disciples who abandoned him in his hour of need? The Christian martyrs of the first and second centuries never saw Jesus Christ and yet believed in him to their death. One can say that their faith and sacrifice was greater than the apostles, as they are depicted in the Bible. From the Muslim point of view, this simply cannot be the case.

In verse 112, God recounts a miracle that the disciples requested. The verse states: **"The apostles said, 'Jesus Son of Mary, can your Lord send us down a feast from heaven?' He said, 'Be wary of God, if you are believers.'"** (Surah 5:112)

Here, we learn that the disciples call him Jesus Son of Mary, and not the son of God or even the son of David. This is a departure of what we find in the Bible. Jesus' initial response was to admonish them to fear God and not make such requests. The request of miracles was a common practice of non-believing Jews of the time. The intention of some Jews was not to affirm their faith but to test the prophets of God. However, the request of the disciples was not intended to test Jesus, but to reaffirm their own faith in order that they may be witnesses to the truth.

This is clearly evident in verse 113 which states: **"They said, 'We want to partake thereof, so our hearts may be satisfied, and we may know you have told us the truth, and we may be witnesses to it.'"** (Surah 5:113)

Being content with the purpose of the disciples, Jesus Christ prays to God to fulfill the miracle in the next verse.

> **"Jesus Son of Mary said, 'O God, our Lord, send us down a feast from heaven, to be a festival for us, for the first of us and the last of us, and a sign from You. And provide for us, as You are the best of providers.'"** (Surah 5:114)

When a prophet makes such a request, God grants the petition. In this case, God adds a condition. The next verse states:

Chapter 7: Al-Ma'idah (The tablecloth with food)

> **"God said, 'I will indeed send it down to you. But if any of you scoff after that, I will punish him with a torment I have never inflicted on a people.'"** (Surah 5:115)

Even though this miracle is not found in the Bible, it does not preclude its occurrence because the last passage in John's Gospel states that there are signs and miracles that have not been preserved in the Gospels. In John 21:25 it states, "And there are also many other things which Jesus did, which if they were written in detail, I suppose what even the world itself would not contain the books that would be written." In examining this miracle, we can extrapolate that it took place during his last days. We can assert this because verse 114 states **"O God, our Lord, send us down a feast from heaven, to be a festival for us, for the first of us and the last of us."** Jesus Christ's usage of the term "last" suggests that no other disciples were added to his ministry. Also, despite seeing the great miracles performed by Jesus Christ (healing the sick, curing the leprous, raising the dead, etc.), why did the faithful disciples request a tablecloth with food from heaven? In my opinion, this miracle is symbolic of Jesus' return. I believe that when Jesus revealed to his disciples his ascension and future return, the disciples sought comfort and reassurance that God will fulfill the second coming. As such, the table spread was a sign from heaven witnessed by the disciples that made their faith complete and removed any doubt of Jesus' return. It is also my opinion that the container that the food from heaven was placed on is the Holy Grail, the existence of which Christians debate. The word 'grail' is English but it comes from the French word 'greal' which means dish. The special status of the Holy Grail is not just due to the fact that it was used by Prophet Jesus and the disciples during the last supper. After all, every prophet has had a last meal served in their own dish, but no added significance has been placed on them. Thus, the special status of the Holy Grail used by Prophet Jesus is its origin which was the dish that carried the sustenance brought down from heaven as requested by the faithful disciples.

After discussing the faithful, God turns His attention to the most serious transgression against Him. In verse 116, God asks Jesus Christ on the Day of Judgment the following:

> **"And God will say, 'Jesus Son of Mary, did you tell people, 'Take to me and my mother as deities rather than God'? He will say, 'Glory to You! It is not for me to say what I have no right to. If I used to say that, You would have known it.**

You know what is in my essence, while I do not know what is in Your essence. For You are the one who knows all hidden secrets.'"

Then in verse 117, Jesus Christ responds by absolving himself:

"I never told them anything but what You instructed me— 'Worship God, my Lord and your Lord.' And I was a witness to them while I sojourned among them. And when You took me, it was You who were watching over them. And You are witness to all things."

In his response, Jesus Christ emphatically denies ever making such a claim. Nowhere in the Bible do we find Jesus making any claim or insinuation to worship him. In fact, we find the complete opposite. Jesus Christ is the one who is prostrating, supplicating, and bowing in front of God and oftentimes alone. We read in the verse that Jesus Christ reaffirms his own servant status and professes to teach only that which was commanded of him, namely the worship of the One true God. This is confirmed by John 17:8 where Jesus states, "For the words which You gave me I have given to them; and they received them and truly understood that I came forth from You, and they *believed that You sent me.*" Indeed, we find in the Gospels that Jesus Christ teaches the worship of the One God and adhering to the commandments (the first and most important refers to the oneness of God). In Mark 12:29, Jesus states: "Hear, O Israel! The Lord our God is one Lord." Furthermore, in Matthew 19:17, we read that when a man praises Jesus, he replies "Why do you call me good? Only God is good, and if you want to achieve eternal life, then follow the commandments." In this verse, he denies his own divinity when he states "Why do you call me good? Only God is good." He also asserts that eternal life is to be achieved by adhering to the commandments. There is no reference of dying for the sins of man in order to be saved. Despite these assertions, Christians did go astray. But as we learn in the Quranic verse, Jesus Christ was a witness over them while he dwelt among them and taught them the straight path. This is also supported by John 17:12, "While I was with them, I was keeping them in Your name which You have given me; and I guarded them and no one of them perished but the son of perdition, so that the Scripture would be fulfilled." However, he absolved himself of any accountability afterwards when God lifted him into heaven. We must remember that even though prophets teach the Divine message, errors and misinterpretations may follow after them. This is the case not only with the divinity of Jesus but also with the worship

Chapter 7: Al-Ma'idah (The tablecloth with food)

of Mary. Even though there isn't a thimble of Biblical support that deifies Mary, Christians in their history have prayed to and even worshiped Mary. This accusation holds true even today.

That being the case, any violation of the first commandment – to worship the One True God – will be judged by God accordingly. In verse 118, Prophet Jesus recognizes the sovereignty and final authority of God to judge his servants, but also acknowledges God's ability to be merciful and forgiving:

"If you punish them, so be it, for they are Your slaves; and if You forgive them, so be it, for You are the Mighty, the Wise."

In verse 119, God responds to Prophet Jesus thusly:

"God will say, 'This is a day on which the sincerity of the sincere profits them; there are gardens for them, below which rivers flow, wherein they will abide forever. God is pleased with them, and they are pleased with God. That is the great attainment."

Muslims believe on the Day of Judgment all people will be brought forth, and will be judged according to all that they had believed and done. This is supported by Matthew 16:27: "For the Son of Man is going to come in the glory of His Father with His angels, and will then repay every man according to his deeds." God will disclose the truth and those that had followed in it will be rewarded with heaven. Those who had disbelieved, disobeyed, and followed the false teachings in addition to having worshipped other Gods will be punished. Muslims believe the ultimate judgment of reward and punishment is ultimately God's. Prophet Jesus will have no authority to decide on this matter because he has absolved himself for the beliefs and practices that his people embraced after his ascension into heaven. This is clearly stated in Matthew 7:22-23: "Many will say to Me on that day, 'Lord, Lord, did we not prophesy in Your name, and in Your name cast out demons, and in Your name perform many miracles? And then I will declare to them, *'I never knew you; DEPART FROM ME, YOU WHO PRACTICE LAWLESSNESS.'*" Moreover, the notion that it is God who will judge the people accordingly and Prophet Jesus will not be an authority is also stated in Timothy. According to 1 Timothy 2:5, "For there is one God, and one mediator also between God and men, the man Christ Jesus." This verse places Prophet Jesus as a mediator not as a final judge or the final authority. Muslims believe all

Prophets will act on behalf of their people to seek God's mercy and forgiveness of their people. However, all people will be judged according to their faith and works and not on the intercession of any prophet.

8

Al-An'am

(The Cattle)

In Surah 6, Al-An'am, or The Cattle, the name of Prophet Jesus appears in verse 85. Al-An'am was revealed in Mecca during 616 CE Revelation at this time was primarily focused upon the oneness of God and Prophet Muhammad being sent as a messenger. As the reader is now well-aware, the Arabs were the descendants of Abraham and Ishmael, and as a result, were once taught the worship of the one God. However, the Arabs, over time, had abandoned these principles and plunged into polytheism. In fact, at the time of Prophet Muhammad, the Arab idolaters had 360 idols, which they housed in the Kabba. However, to their credit, Allah was the one true unseen God, superior to the other gods.

According to God's plan, Prophet Muhammad was sent to the Arabs in order to bring them to the path of God. In verse 83, God reminds the Arabs that Prophet Muhammad is one of many prophets that were sent before him. Through verse 83 to 85, seventeen prophets are named and identified. Although the Arabs considered themselves illiterate and unlearned, they acknowledged the divine guidance of earlier prophets to the Jews and Christians. In fact, the Arabs' respect for them was based upon the recognition that they were God's chosen people, having both the blessings of prophets and scripture. The Arabs never considered that God could or would send a prophet amongst them. They did not feel worthy of this intention, nor did they desire it. They were fully content with the protocol of their forefathers, who worshipped many gods, did not believe in resurrection or the Day of Judgment, heaven or hell, etc.

It is precisely for this reason that God sent Prophet Muhammad, thereby honoring the Abrahamic covenant and reminding the Arabs that Prophet Muhammad is a prophet like many that came before him. In verse 83-86, it states:

"And that was the argument on Our behalf We gave Abraham versus his people. We raise by degrees whomever

We will. For your Lord is most judicious, most intelligent. And We gave him Isaac and Jacob. We guided them all. And We guided Noah before that; and from his descendants David and Solomon, and Jacob and Joseph, and Moses and Aaron. Thus do We recompense those who do good. And Zacharias and John, and Jesus and Elias. Each of them had integrity. And Ishmael and Elisha, and Jonas and Lot; and each of them We blessed over all people."

In verse 85, Jesus is mentioned with Zachariah, John the Baptist, and Elias. Muslims recognize the status of Prophet Jesus as being sent by God as a messenger and prophet. This is consistent with the various biblical passages that identify Prophet Jesus as a prophet. For example, in Mark 6:4 and Matthew 24:19:

"Jesus said to them, "A prophet is not without honor except in his hometown and among his own relatives and in his own household."

"And He said to them, "What things?" And they said to Him, "The things about Jesus the Nazarene, who was a prophet mighty in deed and word in the sight of God and all the people."

Both of the above passages identified Jesus Christ as being a prophet of God. Interestingly, one of the signs of a true prophet is that he is eventually sent into forced migration by his people or city. We see this in cases of Abraham, where he fled Ur; Moses, who fled Egypt; Jesus, who fled Nazareth, and finally Prophet Muhammad, who fled Mecca. One final thought regarding the designation of Prophet: Muslims believe that God had chosen his prophets prior to the creation of Adam. This will be discussed at some length in Surah 33. For now, it should be understood that prophet hood is a designation by the Divine as He communicates through His Angel Gabriel. As such, Muslims believe God completed the line of prophet hood by sending Prophet Muhammad; this is why Prophet Muhammad is known as the Seal of the Prophets.

9

At-Tawba

(The Repentance)

The next verse that discusses Prophet Jesus is found in Surah 9, titled Repentance. This Surah was revealed in Medina around the year 631, shortly after the victory of Mecca. This Muslim victory came eight years after the forced migration of Prophet Muhammad and his followers, leaving behind their families and their belongings. No one at the time could imagine that one man, orphaned and raised by his grandfather, later to become an outcast of his people and tortured for thirteen years could return with the flag of victory, proclaiming the worship of one God.

Prophet Muhammad and ten thousand of his followers arrived in Mecca without resistance from the Arabs; there were virtually no casualties. Prophet Muhammad did not retaliate in response to over twenty years of turmoil that the Meccan Arabs wrought. Moreover, those Arabs who did not want to accept Islam were not harmed. On the contrary, they were protected by earlier treaties. This Surah does contain certain passages that are used against Muslims to promulgate the teaching that the Quran commands the killing of infidels.

This type of casual reading of the Quran is not appropriate and leads to misinterpretation. It is imperative to know when and under what circumstances a particular passage was revealed. The implementation of such passages was based upon certain conditions. Upon capturing Mecca, Prophet Muhammad reclaimed the worship of one God, and removed all idols from the Kabba. As such, he maintained the sanctity of Mecca, ordering all idol worshippers who did not choose to accept Islam to leave the city within four months or until their treaties with the Muslims expired. If they refused to leave, then the Muslims had the order to expel them from the holy city. It is clear that Prophet Muhammad honored earlier treaties, despite having captured the Arab capital.

In fact, the year that Mecca was reclaimed for the Abrahamic faith, both Muslims and idolaters worshipped in the city together. However, this was the last and only time that a non-Muslim could enter into Mecca. The same is true of Medina, where the tomb of Prophet Muhammad is located. Muslims considered both Mecca and Medina the two holy cities in which Islam has been the only religion practiced for over 1400 years. The application of this passage or any other passage which calls for the killing of non-Muslims is unacceptable.

In verse 30, God recounts a sin attributed to the Jews and Christians when they proclaim that God has sons. Verse 30 states:

"The Jews call Ezra son of God, and the Christians call the Messiah son of God. That is what they say with their mouths; they imitate the words of those who scoffed before. May God fight them; how deceived they are!"

Thus far, we have thoroughly discussed the Muslim position that rejects the mainstream Christian belief that Jesus is the Son of God. It is incompatible and stands in contradiction to the first commandment. Declaring a messenger of God to the status of being the son of God had also been the practice of the Jews.

If we examine the Old Testament, it becomes rather clear that throughout their history, the Jews have engaged in idol worship. The idols represented sons and daughters of the divine. Islam denounces this pagan belief adopted by the Jews, and later, Christians. To their credit, the Jewish people today do not interpret the title of Son of God literally, as the Christians do with Jesus Christ. The use of the phrase "son of God" in the Bible refers to angels and the superhuman.

For example, in Genesis 6:2 and 6:4, the phrase "sons of God" is used to refer to angels. Also, in the New Testament (Matthew 5:9), the peacemakers are referred to as "sons of God." In both cases, the phrase, "sons of God," does not imply divinity. For the sake of consistency, Christians must reconcile the obvious misinterpretation of this phrase. Certainly, Christians would reject the earlier Jewish position - as posited by the Muslims - that Ezra was the son of God. Likewise, the Jews would reject the Christian belief that Jesus Christ is the Son of God. In both of these cases, the Quran repeatedly and categorically denies these dogmas. Muslims, since the very beginning, have upheld the oneness of God without any associations.

10

Maryam

(Mary)

The next significant set of verses concerning Prophet Jesus appears in Surah 19 entitled "Maryam." Interestingly, the Quran and not the Bible has a chapter named for Maryam and provides a detailed account of her conception, family background, and upbringing. As mentioned in our discussion of Surah 3, Maryam's parents desired a child in their old age to continue the family tradition of service to the Holy Temple in Jerusalem. The conception of Maryam was miraculous because both parents had reached old age. As such, when Maryam's mother became pregnant, their expectation was that God would bestow a son to continue this legacy as was the Jewish custom at the time. Also, Surah 3 describes how she was embraced by her community as everyone wanted to be her caretaker. As we know, Prophet Zachariah was divinely selected and became her caretaker. This narrative is nowhere to be found in the Bible or any other Christian text. This flies in the face of those who accuse Prophet Muhammad of plagiarism and for copying the stories directly from the Old and New Testaments. The reader should keep this in mind as we begin to discuss Surah 19 since this Surah provides more details about John and Jesus that are nowhere to be found elsewhere.

Surah Maryam was revealed approximately four and a half to five years after prophet hood (614-615) making it a relatively early Surah. At the time, there were few converts to the nascent Muslim community and persecution began to appear at an intolerable level. Embargos and sanctions were imposed by the polytheists, people were lashed and tortured, and laborers would not be paid their wages unless they denounced Islam, and so forth. It was during this time that Prophet Muhammad encouraged some of his community to flee to Abyssinia. This Christian nation was ruled by a righteous king named Najjashi who was celebrated for his justice and tolerance. During the fifth year of prophet hood, approximately 70 Muslims secretly fled to Abyssinia. The pagan leadership in Mecca soon dispatched a delegation to retrieve them. They formally brought a case to Najjashi against these 70 Muslims for being religious renegades who needed to be immediately returned to Mecca where they would be prosecuted. Being a just king, Najjashi would not release them without a fair trial because he felt that all religions were once renegades. It was during this hearing that Surah Maryam was instrumental in establishing common ground between Christians and Muslims, which appealed to the sentiments of Najjashi. In fact, after hearing Surah Maryam and the Quranic account of Mary and Jesus, he drew a line on the ground with his staff and proclaimed "The difference between you and us is no thicker than this line." Najjashi allowed the Muslims to take refuge in Abyssinia where they lived for a time until their migration to Medina after the Prophet had established a prosperous and safe Islamic community.

The Surah begins with the account of Prophet Zachariah and his desire for a son as a successor. Surah 19:2-6 states:

> "**A recitation of the mercy of your Lord on the devotee Zacharias. He called on his Lord with a secret cry, saying, 'My Lord, my bones have become feeble, and my hair has turned white, but I have never been disappointed in praying to You. Now I fear my relatives after me, as my wife is barren. So give me a son from You, who will be my heir, and succeed to the lineage of Jacob. And, my Lord, make him acceptable."**

These verses reveal that Prophet Zachariah prayed silently to his Lord who always granted his prayers. Although some of these verses are similar and have been discussed in Surah 3, I would like to highlight some additional points worth mentioning. It is not coincidental that whenever the Quran discusses Prophet Jesus in detail, the story of John the Baptist precedes it or closely follows. The reason is because the birth of John is miraculous because Zachariah was old and feeble and his wife was barren. Accordingly, the birth of Jesus was also miraculous because of the Immaculate Conception. We are told that Zachariah prayed in solitude and his exact words are in the Quran. The only thing that appears in the Bible is found in Luke's Gospel which simply states that Zachariah petitioned his Lord. The circumstances of his prayer, why he wanted a son and the type of heir he requested are not in any other text except the Quran.

Verses 7 through 11 discuss the fact that God accepted his prayer and granted him a son whose name God chose as John.

"O Zacharias: We bring you good news of a son, whose name will be John—Yahya, 'He Lives'—We have not attributed it as a namesake before. He said, 'My Lord, how will I have a son when my wife is barren and I have become decrepit with age?' 'It will be so: your Lord says that is easy for Me, since I created you before, when you had been nothing.' 'My Lord, give me a sign.' 'Your sign shall be that you not speak to people for three nights in a row.' Then he came out from his prayer niche to his people and told them to praise God in the morning and the evening."

Again, it should be mentioned that when Prophet Zachariah earnestly prayed for a son, he knew with certitude that his prayer would be answered as they have always been answered. It is erroneous to interpret that Zachariah doubted his Lord, as is portrayed in the Bible. The Quranic version is clear that Zachariah did not doubt his Lord but simply inquired about how and by what means his request would come to fruition. God replies by asserting that such supplications are easy for Him as He created all creation from nothing aforetime. Zachariah knew that this miracle would come to pass but wanted to ascertain when it would be fulfilled, and in anticipation requested a sign from his Lord. The sign that was given to him was that he could not speak for three days during which he prayed day and night.

Verses 12 – 15 describe the bounty that was bestowed upon John the Baptist through God's grace. He was given: wisdom at a young age, purity of heart, compassion, obedience to his parents, and the fear of God. These divinely endowed characteristics have elevated the status of John, in the eyes of God, and because of it in Islam as well. The Quran preserves the status of John the Baptist as an imminent messenger of God. The followers of John the Baptist were referred to as the Sabians in the Quran. On numerous occasions, the Quran extols the position of the followers of John the Baptist; it says in 2:62: **"The Muslims, the Jews, the Christians, and the Sabians, any who believe in God and the last day and do good have their reward with their Lord. There is nothing for** them to fear; they will not sorrow." Today, the Sabians can be found in places like Iraq, Syria, and certain localities in Lebanon. The Sabians believe in one God and believe that John the Baptist was the teacher of Jesus Christ, and do not establish the divinity of Jesus Christ as the other Christians do. In contrast, the portrayal of John the Baptist in the Bible is initially good but the depiction initially changes after the arrival of Jesus Christ. In the beginning, we are told that John the Baptist is an important messenger of God who would foreshadow the coming of the Anointed One, and after the arrival of Jesus is requested to perform Jesus' baptism. Later on, Jesus Christ himself lowered the status of John and allegedly said, "Truly I say to you, among those born of women there has not arisen anyone greater than John the Baptist! Yet the one who is least in the kingdom of heaven is greater than he." (Matthew 11:11). The Christian view is that John the Baptist questioned the validity of Jesus Christ as the true Messiah, when he said, "Are You the Expected One, or do we look for someone else?" (Luke 7:19) From a Muslim point of view, not only is such a belief fallacious but this quote attributed to Jesus Christ is denied by Muslims as inconsistent and demeaning of a true prophet and messenger of God. The Quran says that God bestowed peace upon John upon his birth, after his death, and when he will be raised again.

> "And mention Mary in the Book: when she withdrew from her people to a place in the East, and secluded herself from them, We sent her Our spirit, which appeared to her just like a man. She said 'I take refuge from you with the Benevolent One, if you are conscientious.' He said, 'I am only a messenger from your Lord, to give you a sinless son.' She said, 'How will I have a son, when no man has touched me and I have not been unchaste?' He said, 'It will be so.' He said, 'Your Lord says, 'It is easy for Me; and We intend to make him a sign for humankind, and a mercy from Us.' So the matter is decided.' So she carried him, secluding herself with him in a faraway place. Then labor pains impelled her to the trunk of a palm tree. She said, 'Would that I had died before this and been completely forgotten!' Then he called to her from below, saying, 'Do not grieve; your Lord has put a stream beneath you, 'and shake the trunk of the palm toward you to let fresh ripe dates fall by you. Then eat and drink and be of good cheer: but if you see any man, say, 'I have dedicated a fast to the Benevolent

Chapter 10: Maryam (Mary)

One, so I shall not talk to any human being today.'" (Surah 19:16-26)

In verse 16, God directs our attention to the narrative of Mary and Jesus. **"And mention Mary in the Book: when she withdrew from her people to a place in the East."**

From this verse, we know that Mary was assigned a room in the Eastern part of the temple where she worshiped in seclusion. If you recall in our discussion of Surah 3 Lady Mary was given to the service of the temple by her parents. This was specified in the previously mentioned verse 16 where she lived in a room in the east. Being assigned a room within the temple under special circumstances is corroborated by the gospel according to Luke in which Anna lived and worshiped within the temple day and night. The verse states "...and then as a widow to the age of eighty four she never left the temple, serving night and day with fasting and prayers" (Luke 2:37).

Interestingly, when God sent Angel Gabriel, he appeared to Lady Mary as a man which caused her to be frightened. In verse 18 she then asks, **"She said 'I take refuge from you with the Benevolent One, if you are conscientious."** If she were a woman of less perfect character her reaction to finding a man in her private quarters may have been very different. Thus the accusation that was leveled by the Jewish establishment was an egregious sin to say the least. We are honored to read in the Quran that she was a person of the highest character. This is why Muslims love and respect her, and when her name is mentioned Muslims say "may God's blessing and peace be upon her!"

Muslims believe that at the time God sent Angel Gabriel, Lady Mary was a young adolescent approximately 10 to 13 years of age. However, Christian scholars estimate that she may have been in her early teens. Nevertheless, at this time she was physically capable of giving birth. Although this narrative of Angel Gabriel giving the news to Lady Mary has been discussed in detail in Surah 3, I do want to clarify what can be a source of confusion for some. In verse 17, God uses the plural **'We sent her Our spirit'** and in other translations **'we sent our angel'** which some Christians have taken to imply that the trinity concept does exist in the Quran. The verse states, **"We sent her Our spirit, which appeared to her just like a man."** To even vaguely insinuate that the notion of the triune God is represented in the Quran is an outright fabrication. Islam came to restore monotheism and to reaffirm the universal commandment that all prophets of God brought, namely the worship of the One God. How then, do Muslims explain this verse? In most languages, including Arabic and English, a speaker or writer will use "we" or "our" while referring to himself. This use of "we" is called the "Royal We". Therefore, when God reveals the Quran in Arabic He uses "We" while maintaining that He is One. Even Arab idolaters who worshipped more than 360 gods never made the claim that God must be plural because the word "we" is used. It should be noted that it is impossible to make the word "Allah" plural. This is something that can be done in English. The word "god" can be made plural by adding an "s" (gods). Also, the word god can be made feminine by adding "dess" (goddess). However, this is impossible to do with the word Allah: this word cannot be made plural and nor can gender be superimposed.

It is also worth mentioning that in some translations of the Quran, the phrase "We sent Our spirit" is used, while other translations use "We sent Our angel." Both are acceptable and valid. The former is a literal translation of the word *Ruh* which is the Arabic word for spirit. On the other hand, the latter identifies the spirit to be Angel Gabriel. This subject needs to be raised because there are again some Christians who use the phrase 'We sent Our spirit' to suggest that the Holy Spirit is somehow divine because it emanates from God. This is categorically false. The Quran repeatedly uses the word spirit to refer to Angel Gabriel. For example, in Surah 97 verse 4 the word *Ruh* is used in the following way: **"The angels and the spirit descend therein, by permission of their Lord, on every matter."** Again, every Muslim scholar has identified this to be Angel Gabriel. Moreover, the use of "the spirit" as source of revelation is corroborated by Zacharias 7:12, "They could not hear the law and the words which the Lord of hosts had sent by His Spirit through the former prophets." Concurrently, no Muslim has ever considered Angel Gabriel to be divine! Therefore the statement "We sent Our spirit" is not taken literally.

In verse 19 Angel Gabriel gave Mary glad tidings that she will bear a son. **"He said, 'I am only a messenger from your Lord, to give you a sinless son.'"** In the next verse, she responds, **'How will I have a son, when no man has touched me and I have not been unchaste?** God replies **"It is easy for Me; and We intend to make him a sign for humankind, and a mercy from Us.' So the matter is decided."** (Surah 19:21).

Here, we read why God is bringing forth a child who will become a prophet in a manner that was never done before (through virgin birth). The answer is found only in the Quran which declares that he will be a sign unto humankind.

Chapter 10: Maryam (Mary)

What does "being a sign unto humankind" truly mean? God created the heavens and the earth and everything in between. Afterwards, He set forth natural laws but he is not bound by those laws. All human beings are created through the joining of the sperm from the male and the egg from the female. However, there are three exceptions to this natural law. Prophet Adam was created without a man and woman. God created Eve by using Adam's rib, and Prophet Jesus was created without a man and only through the woman. Thus, God can create and bring forth human life any way that He chooses. In the first case, creation appeared without a man and woman, in the second case with the man alone, and in the third case using only a woman. Therefore, the creation of Prophet Jesus is a sign unto humankind and representative of God's glory and power. In fact, there are creatures in the animal kingdom that do not require a male's participation. Rather, the female will give birth by herself. This process is referred to as Parthenogenesis which in Greek means virgin creation. If some animals and plants have this capability, then why should virgin creation be a source of disbelief when performed by the Creator of all things?

Moreover, not only is he a sign to man from God, he is also a mercy from Him. The law that the Jewish people were under was very severe. The Torah contained 613 commandments that were made obligatory on the Jewish people. Prophet Jesus was sent with new revelation that was intended to unburden the lives of ordinary Jews. Undoubtedly, living under the Law is very difficult and Orthodox Jews should be commended for their steadfastness. However, God wanted to facilitate religion for them so that they would not live under such austere parameters forever. Thus, He sent Prophet Jesus with the Ingeel (Gospel), and as such, he was a mercy from God to the Jewish people.

To continue, verse 22 states, **"So she carried him, secluding herself with him in a faraway place."** The Quran does not specify the name of this place but describes it. However, the New Testament has Prophet Jesus born in Bethlehem and living in Nazareth. There is an elaborate narrative regarding his birth that chronicles that three magi see a star in the east. They trace the star and come to find baby Jesus in a manger with Mary and Joseph by his side. However, in the Quran we learn that when it came time to give birth Lady Mary went to a secluded area and sought shelter under a date palm. During her labor pains she cries out, **"Would that I had died before this and been completely forgotten!"** (Quran 19:23). Not only is she not forgotten but her words that she spoke at the time are recorded forever in the Quran. In Islam, mothers have a higher status than the father not only because of the agony that they undergo during childbirth, but also the challenges they face during pregnancy and after the child is born. In the famous collection of An-Nasa'i, Prophet Muhammad is recorded to have said, "Paradise is at the feet of the mother." However, all mothers at the time of delivery usually have someone to comfort them. But Lady Mary was facing this ordeal alone in the middle of nowhere. Although she was alone it was God who comforted her and provided her with sustenance. **"And shake the trunk of the palm toward you to let fresh ripe dates fall by you."** (19:25)

In verse 26, God commands Lady Mary to fast by not speaking to anyone. Self-discipline by controlling the tongue used to be a type of fast that people at the time performed. **"Then eat and drink and be of good cheer: but if you see any man, say, 'I have dedicated a fast to the Benevolent One, so I shall not talk to any human being today.'"** God prescribed this fast to protect her from answering questions about the new child. All religions of the world require their followers to fast by abstaining from food, water, and sexual intercourse. However, the Abrahamic traditions teach that refraining from eating and drinking is an incomplete fast if the individual fails to control his tongue from unlawful speech. God is not in need of our fast from food if we verbally abuse his creatures. This is what Lady Mary was told to do. She continued this fast until she brought baby Jesus back to her people. In verse 27 we read **"Finally she carried him to her people: they said, 'Mary, you sure have done an unheard-of-thing!"** It is important to note that Muslims do not have Lady Mary being married to any man prior to the birth of Prophet Jesus. She was by herself when Angel Gabriel brought the news that she will bear a son. She was also alone when she gave birth, and she brought her son to her people on her own. There is no mention in the Quran and Hadith of Joseph or any other man that was married to her.

However, when we examine the Biblical account in Matthew for instance, we read the following narrative. Matthew 1:19-20 is "And Joseph her husband, being a righteous man and not wanting to disgrace her, planned to send her away secretly. But when he had considered this, behold, an angel of the Lord appeared to him in a dream, saying, 'Joseph, son of David, do not be afraid to take Mary as your wife; for the Child who has been conceived in her is of the Holy Spirit." We must assume that they both did marry, but the question is when? If we believe that Joseph took Mary as his wife shortly after his encounter with the angel, then the Jewish accusation that Jesus was born of fornication would be inconsistent. "…They said to Him [Jesus], 'we are not born of fornication" (John 8:41). Obviously, if a husband and wife present a newborn as their child, the issue

Chapter 10: Maryam (Mary)

of illegitimate birth does not arise. Again, the Christian perspective of Mary being betrothed to Joseph does raise doubt about the Immaculate Conception. The Quran makes it clear that it was Mary alone that brought baby Jesus to her people. They responded, **"Mary, you sure have done an unheard-of-thing!" "O sister of Aaron, your father was not a bad man, and your mother was not [unchaste]."** If the child was truly born unholy, then an honorable woman like Mary would at least have been reluctant to present the child to her family. After all, she comes from a distinguished pedigree as she is the descendent of Prophet Aaron and her father was the caretaker of the Holy Temple.

Before we discuss verse 29, the Muslim position is clear: that Jesus was a descendant of Aaron, whereas the Bible claims that Jesus was a descendant of Judah, as a result of his stepfather Joseph. This is ironic, because under Jewish law, there are no rights of inheritance given to a stepchild. Moreover, there is no biblical reference of Mary's genealogy. The Quran, however, identifies both Mary's father and uncle, Zacharias, as priests and descendants of Aaron and Levi.

> **"Now she pointed to him. They said, 'How can we talk to one who is an infant in the cradle?' He said, 'I am indeed the servant of God, who has given me scripture and made me a prophet.'"** (Surah 19:30)

In verse 30, baby Jesus speaks from the cradle, performing the first of many miracles. He spoke these words by the strength of the Holy Spirit. Interestingly, the Quranic account has Jesus' first miracle to be vociferous utterances in defense of his mother, but the New Testament has Jesus turning water into wine as his first miracle. At any rate, in the above verse we see that Jesus identifies himself not only as a servant of God but also a prophet. Such a characterization is confirmed by the Gospels. In Acts, Peter identifies Jesus as a servant even after his ascension. "The God of Abraham, Isaac and Jacob, the God of our Fathers, has glorified His servant Jesus, *the one* whom you delivered and disowned in the presence of Pilate, when he had elected to release Him" (Acts 3:13). This passage confirms that his disciples considered him a servant of God even after his ascension when Christians claim that he became divine. Also in Luke his followers refer to him as a prophet: "The things about Jesus the Nazarene, who was a prophet mighty in deed and word in the sight of God and all the people." (Luke 24:19)

In verse 31 through 33, speaking from the cradle, Prophet Jesus states: **"[God] made me blessed wherever I am; and has prescribed prayer and** charity for me as long as I live, and kindness to my mother as well; and did not make me an arrogant malcontent. And peace is upon me the day I was born, and the day I die, and the day I am resurrected, alive."** From these verses, we see that God had made him blessed which in Greek translates as Christ. Upon careful reflection on these verses, we also observe that prophets of God are expected to perform righteous deeds and are not exempt from them. Prayer, charity, and benevolence to his mother were commanded by God. Again, we read throughout the Gospels that Prophet Jesus is seen praying on numerous occasions. One example, according to Luke 22:45, states "When he rose from prayer and went back to the disciples, he found them sleeping from sorrow." An additional example comes from Matthew 14:23 which states, "After he had sent the crowds away, he went up on the mountain by himself to pray; and when it was evening, he was there alone."

In verse 32 specifically, we read that God commanded Prophet Jesus to be kind to Lady Mary as part of his filial responsibility. Again, if Joseph had been her husband then God would have commanded Prophet Jesus be kind to both of them. Therefore the Muslim position without reservations of any kind is the belief that Mary did not have a husband and was a single mother. Finally, in verse 33 we read that there was peace upon him at his birth, his death and there will be peace when he is raised again. Muslims do not believe that Christ died on the Cross and instead was lifted into heaven. In his second coming he will live on the earth and will die of natural causes. When the Final Hour approaches he along with all sentient beings will pass away and be held accountable on the Day of Judgment.

How do Muslims know such minutia about the lives of both Prophet Jesus and Lady Mary when this level of detail is to be found nowhere? In verse 34, God provides the answer. **"That was Jesus, Son of Mary, a word of truth about which they doubt."** This verse is an affirmation that Prophet Muhammad was a true prophet of God. There have emerged countless disputes and sources of controversy over the years in Christianity on a variety of issues. However, Islam without exception has a singular narrative, since the advent of Islam and until today. After providing such specific information, God singles out an exorbitant sin that emerged as a result of misinformation and disputation. In verse 35, God states: **"Having a son is not attributable to God, who is beyond that, and when having determined something merely says to it, 'Be,' and it is."** Islam, through the Quran and the teachings of Prophet Muhammad, rejects the Christian belief that Jesus Christ is the son of God who shares in his divinity. God does not beget a son because His glory and majesty is far removed from this act. It is quite reprehensible to accuse Almighty God of being in any way connected with such sexual matters. As a result, some newer versions of the New Testament have replaced "begotten" with "one and only son." If your particular Bible does contain the word begotten, then ask yourself whether the God that you worship is capable of such an act. The reality is that God is quite capable of creating Prophet Jesus by His word, as He did with Prophet Adam whom no Christian would claim was begotten by God. This divine utterance "Be" can be found in the first chapter of Genesis in which "Be" repeatedly appears. The Christian belief articulated in Luke 1:35 is rejected by Muslims. "The Holy Spirit will come upon you, and the power of the Most High will overshadow you; and for that reason the holy Child shall be called the Son of God." It is from these types of verses that Christians have extrapolated this convoluted position that Mary was the daughter of the Father, the spouse of the Holy Spirit, and the mother of God. In response to such claims, God revealed Surah 112 which reads: **"Say, 'It is God, unique, God the eternal, not begetting or begotten, not having any equal."**

11

Al-Ahzab

(The Coalition)

The next verse which discusses Prophet Jesus is found in Surah 33, titled Al-Ahzab, or The Coalition. It received this name from The Battle of the Trench, which took place in approximately 627CE; in this battle, the Meccan Arabs established an army of ten thousand, collected from the various Arab tribes. This battle was an incredible test of faith during overwhelming uncertainty. The Muslims had been informed that a large, well-equipped army was marching towards them. With consultation from his followers, Prophet Muhammad ordered the Muslims to dig trenches around Medina, in order to fortify the city. Medina's geography allowed for a defensive position, as the city was protected by large date farms on one side and mountains on the other. Thus, by digging these trenches, the city became virtually impenetrable. Even as the Arab army saw that the Muslims would not engage in battle, they set up camps and surrounded Medina for thirty days, hoping for a Muslim surrender. The Arabs returned to Mecca after severe weather began to rain down on them, leaving even their possessions behind. Having successfully withstood the strongest Arab army, the Muslim defensive victory reverberated throughout the Arab peninsula. Although the thirty day standoff was a tremendous ordeal, filled with fear and doubt, the battle of the trenches strengthened Muslim faith and resolve. Soon thereafter, the Arab idolaters were demoralized, later negotiating the 628 Treaty of Hudabiya, which Prophet Muhammad accepted. The Battle of the Trench was a good indication that Muslims were not aggressors. On the contrary, most of the battles led by Prophet Muhammad were defensive in nature, or fought for some greater good.

In verses 7 and 8, God says, **"And We accepted their covenant from the prophets, and from you, and from Noah and Abraham, and Moses and Jesus Son of Mary: We took an inviolable covenant from them that God may question the truthful about their truth; and God has prepared**

Chapter 11: Al-Ahzab (The Coalition)

a painful penalty for the scoffers." The following discussion regarding this passage assumes basic Muslim belief regarding human creation. Muslims believe, along with Jews and Christians that Adam was created by clay or dirt, and God blew his spirit in it, giving him life. All human beings consist of the spirit and physical flesh. After Adam's creation, Muslims believe, God created the spirits of all his offspring. This is a point of difference between Christians and Muslims. Although the Bible does not provide discourse on human ensoulment, we can extrapolate from both the creation of Adam and Eve that their spirits could only have been created prior to their physical bodies. Similarly, every child of Adam lives as spirit until he or she is joined with their respective mother's fetus on the fourth month. In verse 7, God recounts an oath that was taken by his chosen prophets before they were each joined with a body. According to the verse, this oath was taken by all prophets, including Prophet Muhammad, Noah, Abraham, Moses, and Jesus. Before we discuss the oath, it is necessary to understand that God can only choose those who are able to fulfill the conditions of the oath. That is, they must be trustworthy, truthful, righteous, and persons of excellent character. God would not allow the sinful to be the carriers of His message. One of the criticisms that Muslims have regarding the credibility of the Bible is in reference to the characterization of God's chosen messengers. Upon reading the Bible, one might be left to wonder why God would choose prophets whom engage in egregious and sinful acts. Muslims reject those passages which demean the moral standing of prophets.

Moreover, as prophets, they are duty-bound to deliver the divine message and teachings to their communities. This embodies the nature of the oath. In addition to delivering a divine message, they must demonstrate complete faith as an example to the people, for prophets are the only means by which God communicates to us. If messengers of God waver in their mission, then God's establishment of the Day of Judgment is compromised; God's revelations are rendered incredulous, and the accountability of the people cannot be justly warranted. Muslims believe that every prophet possessed exemplary character in faith, morals, and deeds. Above all, they fulfilled the duties of their prophet hood, a responsibility to deliver divine guidance to the people, risking even death. Moreover, God's prophets will be questioned on the Day of Judgment, as stated in verse 8, **"God may question the truthful about their truth,"** a reference to the questioning of prophets and their faithful devotees. This is corroborated in Surah 5, verse 109: **"One day God will gather the messengers and say, 'What was the response that you were given?' They will say, 'We have no**

knowledge, it is You who know all hidden secrets.'" Although the prophets answer in generalities, as stated in the latter part of verse 109, the questioning implies that they fulfilled their duties in delivering the divine message. It is proper that God asks, **"What was the response that you were given?"**

12

Az-Zukhruf

(The Golden Adornments)

Surah Zukhruf in Arabic means "Golden Adornments" and was revealed in Mecca. As stated earlier, Meccan Surahs were revealed at a time when the situation of Muslims was tenuous, as they were surrounded by idolaters who constantly schemed to eradicate the followers of this nascent religion. Because of this, Surahs revealed in Mecca do not contain injunctions or prohibitions on complex matters. Instead, these Surahs emphasize the core beliefs of the faith including the oneness of God, the After Life, resurrection day, and the stories of previous prophets. Although the Arabs were descendants of Prophet Ishmael, they had for centuries engaged in idol worship. Their religion consisted of worshiping the 360 idols housed in the Kabba. Historically, idols were introduced by various tribes because it was felt that housing these idols in such a sacred place would provide good luck and increase worldly provisions. Over time, the idols became a primary source of revenue for the Meccan Arabs as people came to pay homage to these idols.

Prophet Muhammad was sent to restore the worship of the one God and declared these idols to be unworthy of worship. The Arab leadership took this as a threat to their authority and livelihood. The Quran implored these idolaters to renounce their false gods whom they and their forefathers had prayed to for centuries. The vast majority of them refused to do so, especially the rich and powerful who had the most to lose. After all, their rank in Arab society would be undermined if all the idols were replaced by the worship of an unseen God. Nevertheless, the Quran sought to convince the idolaters that it is God who created the heavens and the earth and all things in between. It is He who is the source of all life and the provider of all things like water, air, light, food, shelter, and so forth. In contrast, the false gods that the Arabs worshiped could not hear or see, and nor were they capable of creating any living thing.

Christ Jesus, The Son of Mary: A Muslim Perspective

In Surah 22:73 God states, **"People, an example is set forth, so listen to it: those to whom you pray instead of God could not create a fly, even if they all cooperated at it. And if a fly should snatch anything from them, they would not recover it from it. The seeker is weak, and so is the sought."**

This verse explicitly argues in a rational and logical manner why gods made out of stone and wood should not be worshipped. Similarly, God suggests they consult the teachings of past Prophets to answer a specific question. In Surah 43:45 God states, **"And ask of Our messengers, whom We sent before you; have We established gods to be worshipped other than the Benevolent One?"** When this verse was revealed, the Arab idolaters retorted by claiming that the Christians worshiped Jesus Christ, who was a messenger of God. In other words, the Arabs invoked the example of Jesus being worshiped by Christians to justify their worship of idols. However, the questioning of earlier prophets in this verse should be read as a challenge to examine previous scriptures since they are what remain after the death of prophets. The prevalence of various practices by a religious community are not de facto proof of the true teachings of prophets of God. Through a closer inspection of Biblical passages, nowhere is there an assertion by Jesus that his followers should worship him.

In verse 57, God responds to the Arab idolaters who raise the issue of Prophet Jesus. **"And when the son of Mary is held up as an example, behold, your people oppose."** By bringing up the example of Prophet Jesus, the Arab idolaters speciously misused analogy to justify their false beliefs. They proved to be argumentative and were not sincerely seeking the truth. This is affirmed in verse 58 which states, **"'Are our gods better, or is he?' They have only set this forth to you to be argumentative; indeed, they are contentious people."** And in verse 59, we read that he is no more than a servant and Prophet of God who received many gifts in the form of miracles. Verse 59 clearly states, **"He was just a servant, whom We blessed and made an example to the Israelites."** We discussed earlier how Jesus Christ was an example by virtue of his miraculous conception and that no one else has been created in this fashion (virgin giving birth). Just as God has the power to create Prophet Jesus without a father, we read in verse 60 that God is capable of producing angels in humankind. In this verse God says, **"Were it Our wish, We would have made angels from among you to act as deputies on earth."** In verse 61, we learn that Prophet Jesus will return before the Day of Judgment. It reads, **"But as for him, he was a sign of the end of time; so do not doubt it, and follow Me: this is a straight path."**

Chapter 12: Az-Zukhruf (The Golden Adornments)

Like Christians, Muslims unanimously believe that Prophet Jesus will come back to the Earth and live out the remainder of his life. He will rule on Earth and there will be peace and joy during his time of reign. Prior to his arrival, there will be bloodshed, worldwide scarcity and monopolization of the global food supply, oppression, and the advent of the anti-Christ who will be a peacemaker among rival nations. After acquiring global dominance, he will demand that he be worshipped. Refusal to do so will lead to the starvation of those communities who will be victims of his boycott. The first of his believers will be the Jews who would be convinced that he is the Christ. He will have demonic power to control the weather, heal the sick, and raise the dead. However, there will be a small group of Muslims that will recognize him as the anti-Christ and will resist his rule. It will be during one of these battles that the true Christ and Messiah, Prophet Jesus, will return and destroy him. Some Protestant denominations have actually believed that the anti-Christ will be the Pope. Muslims reject such a charge because the anti-Christ will be supported by satanic forces whereas the Pope represents the embodiment of the New Testament. However, Muslims and many Christians believe the anti-Christ will likely be Jewish. The anti-Christ's Jewish heritage will likely contribute to a large Jewish following. Nevertheless, Prophet Jesus will return to earth and establish a just kingdom after destroying the anti-Christ and his followers.

One final thought regarding the second coming of Prophet Jesus is the Christian concept of Rapture. As discussed earlier, the Evangelical approach to the Rapture is relatively new which says that Jesus will lift the believers, both dead and alive, into heaven. After this event, there will be seven years of tribulation. Then, Jesus will return and establish a new Israel and a Jewish Kingdom that will last for a thousand years. According to this calculation, it seems that Prophet Jesus will emerge two times, which is inconsistent because it is believed by Muslims that he will only reappear once.

There are numerous details about the signs of the final Hour that are found in Hadith collections. These include the following:

> Narrated by Abu Huraira: "The Prophet (peace be upon him) said: There is no prophet between me and him, that is, Jesus (peace be upon him). He will descend (to the earth). When you see him, recognize him: a man of medium height, reddish hair, wearing two light yellow garments, looking as if drops were falling down from his head though it will not be wet. He will

fight the people for the cause of Islam. He will break the cross, kill swine, and abolish jizyah. God will perish all religions except Islam. He will destroy the Antichrist and will live on the earth for forty years and then he will die. The Muslims will pray over him'" (Sunan Abu Dawud, Book 37, Verse 4310).

Narrated by Abu Huraira: "The Prophet said, 'The Hour (Day of Judgment) will not be established till your wealth increases so much so that one will be worried, for no one will accept his Zakat and the person to whom he will give it will reply, 'I am not in need of it'" (Sahih Bukhari, Book 24, Hadith 493).

Narrated by Anas: "I will narrate to you a Hadith I heard from God's Prophet and none other than I will tell you of it. I heard God's Prophet saying, "From among the portents of The Hour are the following: Religious knowledge will be taken away; General ignorance (in religious matters) will increase; illegal Sexual intercourse will prevail: Drinking of alcoholic drinks will prevail. Men will decrease in number, and women will increase in number, so much so that fifty women will be looked after by one man'" (Sahih Bukhari, Book 62, Hadith 158).

Narrated by Abu Huraira: "God's Prophet said, "When honesty is lost, then wait for The Hour." It was asked, "How will honesty be lost, O God's Prophet?" He said, "When authority is given to those who do not deserve it, then wait for The Hour'" (Sahih Bukhari, Book 76, Hadith 503).

Narrated by Abu Huraira: "God's Prophet said, 'The Hour will not be established till the sun rises from the west, and when it rises (from the west) and the people see it, then all of them will believe (in God). But that will be the time when 'No good it will do to a soul to believe then. If it believed not before...'" (6.158) The Hour will be established (so suddenly) that two persons spreading a garment between them will not be able to finish their bargain, nor will they be able to fold it up. The Hour will be established while a man is carrying the milk of his she-camel, but cannot drink it; and The Hour will be established when someone is not able to prepare the tank to water his livestock

Chapter 12: Az-Zukhruf (The Golden Adornments)

from it; and The Hour will be established when some of you has raised his food to his mouth but cannot eat it'" (Bukhari, Book 76, Hadith 513).

Coming back to the verses, Satan attempts to divert human beings from God in verse 62 which states, **"And don't let Satan divert you, for he is an open enemy to you."** Satan is a self-declared enemy of human beings who is not a rival to God but a rival to man. This is an important distinction between Christianity and Islam since Islam teaches that God Almighty has no rival. Created beings cannot establish rivalry to the Creator. The Quran teaches that Satan seeks a respite on earth for a while with the sole intent to deceive and misguide human beings. However, God desires that His creation be rightly guided and sends prophets and scriptures to lead people to the straight path. In verse 63, God states: **"When Jesus came with clarifications, he said, 'I have brought you wisdom, and come to clarify for you some of what you differ about. So be wary of God, and obey me.'"** One reason why Prophet Jesus was sent to the Children of Israel was to resolve the contradictory teachings and practices that existed at the time. For example, the Jewish authority took advantage of the people by claiming that certain actions were in accordance to the sacred law. This was a clear lie on their part and in fact they failed to live up to their own teachings that they promulgated. In Matthew 21:13 Jesus renounces the activities of the money exchangers, saying, "It is written, 'my house shall be called a house of prayer'; but you are making it a robbers' den."

Moreover, there were two main Jewish groups who had contradictory beliefs and practices. They were the Sadducees and Pharisees. The Sadducees did not believe in the Day of Judgment, the physical resurrection, or angels; whereas the Pharisees upheld the complete opposite teachings on these issues. Hence, Prophet Jesus was sent to clarify these disputed matters. However, like Prophet Muhammad, Jesus faced similar opposition in the form of a misguided elitist establishment. The Jewish authority refused to relinquish its power. This is corroborated by Matthew 21:23 which states, "When he entered the temple, the chief priests and the elders of the people came to him while he was teaching, and said, 'By what authority are you doing these things, and who gave you this authority?" When Prophet Jesus attempted to guide the people from their false beliefs, he faced strong resistance. As the Quran says, Jesus implored his people to **"be wary of God, and obey me."** But of course, the Jewish establishment did not care to obey Prophet Jesus and nor did they fear God. Instead, they plotted to kill him.

In verse 64, Prophet Jesus is quoted as saying, **"It is God that is my Lord and your Lord; so worship God—this is a straight path."** It is clear that Prophet Jesus' teachings and actions reflected the worship of his Creator. At a fundamental level, the relationship that we have with God is the same relationship of Lord and servant that Jesus Christ had with God. And a Lord and a slave can never be coequal, and the One worshiped and the worshiper can never be the same.

13

Al-Hadid[1]

(The Iron)

The next set of verses that discuss Prophet Jesus can be found in Surah Hadid. The word Hadid literally means iron, which appears in verse 25: **"We have sent Our messengers with clear proofs, and We sent the Book and the Balance with them, that humanity may stand by justice. And We sent iron, in which is violent force and advantages for humanity, that God may know who will help God and God's messengers, albeit unseen. God is truly powerful, almighty."** From this verse, we learn that Iron is an element that had been sent down to earth from outer space. Not surprising to Muslims, scientists have determined that the iron on earth originated in space and came down as a result of a supernova (a star that exploded). In fact, there are numerous scientific references in the Quran that span a wide range of disciplines including biology, zoology, embryology, astronomy, physics, and so forth. Since the Quran is the final revelation from God, it contains proofs that have been corroborated by science to establish its authenticity. There has been extensive written documentation of various passages of the Quran that are validated by science. For example, the Big Bang theory has been embraced by the scientific community to explain the origin of the universe. One interpretation of the theory holds that the universe was created in the absence of space and time. This was stated in the Quran over 1400 years ago in Surah 21. The verse states, **"...Your Lord is the Lord of the Heavens and the earth, He who created them from *nothing*: and I am a witness to this Truth"**. Another example of a scientific truth that was revealed to Prophet Muhammad is stated in Surah 51 in the following verse: **"And it is We who have built the universe with [Our creative] power; and, verily, it is *We who are steadily expanding it*"**.

---

[1] It should be noted that within this Surah, the Yusuf Ali translation of the Holy Quran is preferred over the Thomas Cleary translation, as it is more congruous with the original Arabic text.

Prior to the 1920s, most scientific theories suggested that the universe was stagnant. But due to the observations of Edwin Hubble this theory has been disproved. It is now a scientific fact that the universe is expanding as stated in the Quran over 1400 years ago. There are numerous other examples that can be cited, but this would distract us from our central task.

Jesus Christ is mentioned in verse 27 of this Surah. But in verse 26, God mentions two important prophets, Noah and Abraham. **"And We sent Noah and Abraham, and established in their line prophet hood and Revelation: and some of them were on right guidance. But many of them became rebellious transgressors."** Both Noah and Abraham have a high status among God's prophets. It was from Prophet Noah's family lineage that all of God's subsequent prophets originated until Abraham. Muslims believe that Abraham is considered to be the father of the prophets because all remaining prophets were his descendants. However, God sending prophets does not assure that the prophets will be successful in bringing the people to the path of God. It is apparent in verse 26 that the vast majority of the people were transgressors, and only a small minority indeed believed in them. Verse 27 states,

> **"Then, in their wake, We followed them up with (others of) Our prophets: We sent after them Jesus the son of Mary, and bestowed on him the Gospel; and We ordained in the hearts of those who followed him Compassion and Mercy. But the Monasticism which they invented for themselves, We did not prescribe for them: (We commanded) only the seeking for the Good Pleasure of God but that they did not foster as they should have done. Yet We bestowed, on those among them who believed, their (due) reward, but many of them are rebellious transgressors."**

In verse 27, God reestablishes that Jesus Christ had received revelation. What is remarkable about this verse that had not been mentioned in previous verses relates to how the followers of Jesus Christ are portrayed. His followers, and not just the twelve Apostles, are described in the Quran as compassionate and merciful, and these qualities the Quran asserts have been placed by God in their hearts. This depiction is found nowhere in the New Testament. Indeed we find contrary snapshots where the Disciples are described in some Biblical verses as unfaithful and cowardly. If we apply this verse to our modern day context, we would find that Christians are among the most philanthropic people on earth.

Chapter 13: Al-Hadid (The Iron)

Today's Christians are among the most charitable people who freely give their time and wealth to the disenfranchised communities of the world.

However, it seems that a group of early Christians began to practice monasticism. Monasticism is a form of religious life that follows the principles of celibacy and self-imposed depravity. One form, namely eremitic monasticism, is a practice where the individuals are called to live as hermits in the desert. Such practices were not made obligatory on Prophet Jesus' followers. The reason why some chose a monastic lifestyle was their desire to please God. However, this type of a lifestyle is not natural and thus cannot be sustained. Islam prohibits this approach to life. Islam teaches the value of living a responsible life and the performance of doing good to creation as a way to show gratitude to the Creator. Moreover, engaging in permissible pleasures in due moderation allows us the opportunity to express our thankfulness to God for His blessings. The blessings of a family, a home, dressing well are all gifts from God for which the servant is eternally indebted. In contrast, the monastic lifestyle practiced by early Christians was austere to say the least. They used to deprive themselves of the most natural instincts including eating, drinking, sleeping, bathing, grooming, and even wearing appropriate clothing. This is clearly not in keeping with Jesus Christ's teachings. In fact, this was not the practice of his followers as his Disciples worked, married, and had families of their own.

Like earlier prophets, he taught the virtue of worshiping the One God and adhering to His commandments. But most of them eventually went astray. Muslims believe that the immediate followers of Prophet Jesus were truthful to his teachings. However, at some point, the Gospel given to Prophet Jesus was lost and disputes erupted amongst the Christians. They became divided on the most basic issues including who was Jesus, how much of the law should be adhered to, what scripture was acceptable in the various churches, and so forth. It took nearly four centuries to sort through these divisions and those churches that had power and influence began to superimpose their dogma and creed. Muslims believe that the early ecumenical councils of Nicea and Constantinople led to the repression of early Christian beliefs and practices that were taught by Prophet Jesus. God sent Prophet Muhammad with the final revelation to teach not only the Meccan idolaters but also people of other faiths including Christians and Jews.

In verse 28 we read **"O ye that believe! Fear God, and believe in His Messenger, and He will bestow on you a double portion of His Mercy: He will provide for you a Light by which ye shall walk (straight in your path), and**

He will forgive you (your past): for God is Oft- Forgiving, Most Merciful." This verse promises those who believe and follow the teachings of Prophet Muhammad a double reward. Christians who accept Prophet Muhammad as the final prophet of God are blessed with two rewards, because they are believers in both Prophet Jesus as well as Prophet Muhammad. Verse 28 ends with God asserting that He is Most Forgiving, Most Merciful. God effaces all previous sins when the believer turns to Him in repentance and obedience. Muslims believe that the greatest characteristic of God is His boundless mercy. It is through one's contrite repentance that the servant is cleansed of all sins and is brought closer to God. Prophet Muhammad taught the value of seeking God's forgiveness over seventy times a day. This supplication does not entail an intercessor as taught by the Catholic Church. Like all of God's attributes, His mercy is infinite. Hence, when anyone enters the fold of Islam, all previous sins are forgiven. And that person continues to rely on God's mercy both in this world and the Hereafter.

> **"O my Servants who have transgressed against their souls! Despair not of the Mercy of God: for God forgives all sins: for He is Oft-Forgiving, Most Merciful."** (Surah 39:53)

14

As-Saff

(The Rows)

As indicated above, the word As-Saff refers to the rows or ranks during combat. This Surah was revealed in Medina shortly after the battle of Uhud in which the Muslims were defeated. Uhud was a mountain on the outskirts of Medina where this battle took place between the Meccan Arab idolaters and the Muslims. It was the Arab idolaters that traveled over 200 miles to seek retribution for the battle they had lost a year prior--the battle of Badr. Badr was the first battle in Islam between the Muslims and the Arab unbelievers. It occurred during the second year after the migration (624 CE) to Medina in which 313 Muslims defeated the 1000 person strong Arab army. Prior to this battle, Muslims lived in Mecca for 13 years under severe persecution. The conditions were so unbearable that Muslims left their Meccan homeland. Some took refuge in Abyssinia (modern day Ethiopia). Soon afterwards, the people of Medina invited Prophet Muhammad and his followers to establish a Muslim community in Medina. Approximately two years after the migration, Prophet Muhammad received revelation that declared war on Arab idolaters. This declaration resulted in the battle of Badr. **"Victims of aggression are given license because they have been done injustice; and God is well able to help them."** (Surah 22:39)

With this humiliating defeat the Meccan idolaters vowed to return one year later to exact retribution. Prophet Muhammad and his followers set up camp at Uhud and prepared for war. The Meccan Arabs eventually came and even though the Muslims had the upper hand initially and were close to victory, the tides turned against them when they left a key defensive position. A group of Arab idolaters fighting on horseback came around the mountain and attacked the Muslims from behind. In short, the Muslims witnessed defeat for the first time and lost approximately seventy precious followers.

Since we are on the subject of war and the misunderstood concept of Jihad, there is a horrible myth propagated by some Christian writers that requires clarification. These Christians have historically claimed that Muslims are commanded to kill every Christian, Jew, and infidel. They take various Quranic verses out of context in order to perpetuate this stereotype. My second book, God willing, will fully explore this topic. But a few noteworthy comments are necessary. If such a claim was indeed true (that Muslims are ordered to kill non-Muslims), then there would be virtually no non-Muslim communities in Muslim lands. However, there are thriving Christian communities throughout the Muslim world who have lived in relative harmony with their Muslim neighbors. Percentage-wise, there are more Christians living in the Middle East than there are Muslims living in Europe, the United States, and Canada combined (see Appendix). Moreover, if God had commanded Muslims to kill Christians and Jews, how can we explain that Jews and Christians fled to Muslim territories during the Inquisition? There are churches and synagogues that predate Islam which are still preserved and protected in accordance with the Quran. Also, due to historical enmities between Jewish and Christian leaders in Jerusalem over ownership of the Church of the Nativity, both parties have turned to Muslims to be their mediators and have given the keys of the Church to Muslims. Muslims consider the Jews and Christians to be People of the Book and are permitted to marry their women. In fact, this has been made permissible so as to safeguard monotheistic ties that go back to Abraham. In Surah 5, Verse 5 it states: **"And so are chaste believing women, and chaste women from among those to whom scripture was given before you."**

That being said, the primary obstacle that the Muslims faced in Arabia at the time was the Meccan idolaters. Of Prophet Muhammad's 10 years in Medina, a great majority of the battles were fought against them and not the Jews and Christians. This Surah was revealed so as to strengthen the resolve of the Muslims after their defeat at Uhud. In verse 5 of this Surah, God cites the historical example of the Jewish people to teach the Muslims the importance of obedience and steadfastness.

> **"Moses said to his people, 'Why do you injure me when you know I am God's messenger to you?' And when they deviated, God let their hearts become perverse, as God does not guide people who are dissolute. And Jesus Son of Mary said, 'O Children of Israel, I am God's messenger to you, confirming the truth of the Torah before me, and heralding**

Chapter 14: As-Saff (The Rows)

a messenger who will come after me, his name Ahmad, most praiseworthy.' But when he brought them proofs, they said, 'This is obvious sorcery!' And who is more wrong than one who invents falsehood against God even as he is invited to acquiesce; as God does not guide people doing wrong."

Two important thoughts come to mind concerning the above verses. First and foremost, there is an unfair assessment that the Quran is anti-Jewish. This is simply not the case. If we compare Biblical verses that discuss the Jewish people with Quranic ones, the verses in the Bible are far more denigrating and damning. Being the final revelation, the Quran discusses narratives of earlier prophets to teach humanity important lessons of right and wrong. These stories provide important lessons so that such mistakes in faith and judgment can be avoided. Additionally, as mentioned earlier, these Quranic narratives provide greater detail of events than previous scriptures and serve as an important corrective to the false accounts contained in earlier writings. For instance, the insulting sexual depictions of Noah, Lot, Solomon, and David in the Bible are disregarded as fabrications. The same can be said about the false portrayal of Abraham worshipping idols. The truth of these prophets of God and their character are recorded in the Quran. Since God sent more messengers to the Sons of Jacob, we have more details about them. Muslims believe that God sent over 125,000 prophets to the Jewish community. The most celebrated and well known was Prophet Moses. Despite knowing that Prophet Moses was sent by God, the Jewish people nevertheless disobeyed and ridiculed him. Even more reprehensible is the fact that they did this after Moses freed them from 400 years of enslavement. Thus, it was due to their unbelief that God turned their hearts. Verse 5 states, **"Moses said to his people, 'Why do you injure me when you know I am God's messenger to you?' And when they deviated, God let their hearts become perverse, as God does not guide people who are dissolute"**.

As is clear from the verse, God turned their hearts because of what they did and not because they were Jews. After all Moses, Aaron, Joshua, Solomon, and Jesus were all Jews and descendants of Jacob. So in the story of Moses we have the first account of Jewish rebellion against the first major prophet sent to them. In verse 6 we see a similar type of response with the last prophet sent to them, namely Jesus Christ. Verse 6 states, **"And Jesus Son of Mary said, 'O Children of Israel, I am God's messenger to you, confirming the truth of the Torah before me, and heralding a messenger who will come after me, his** name Ahmad, most praiseworthy.' But when he brought them proofs, they said, 'This is obvious sorcery!'"

It is clear from this verse that Prophet Jesus claimed to be a prophet of God and demonstrated his truthfulness by performing the various miracles. God performs the miracles through prophets in order that observers can become true believers. However, those whose hearts were hardened disbelieved due to their pride and arrogance, and they dismissed these miracles as mere sorcery and magic. This was the same charge leveled against Prophet Muhammad when he performed his numerous miracles. These miracles are well documented in the Quran and the various Hadith collections. The dismissal of such clear signs and miracles is a deliberate act of disobedience and it is also a direct rejection of the prophet who performs it. In other words, the rejection of miracles performed by a prophet is a repudiation of not only the prophet but God who sent him. In verse 7 God responds harshly to the Jews who mistook these miracles as sorcery because it is God who performs miracles through prophets. It says, **"And who is more wrong than one who invents falsehood against God even as he is invited to acquiesce; as God does not guide people doing wrong."**

Verse 7 should not be read to suggest that Prophet Jesus is somehow God. After all it should be clear from verse 6 that Prophet Jesus identified himself as a prophet. In rejecting Prophet Jesus' miracles, God treats it to be a rejection of Himself.

Also in verse 6, the observant reader may have noticed the Quranic claim that Prophet Jesus foretells the coming of a prophet whose name will be Ahmad. Ahmad is the root from which we get Muhammad and the two names are interchangeable. In chapter two we had discussed numerous verses of the Old and New Testaments that foreshadowed the coming of Prophet Muhammad. They included the following:

"Declaring the end from the beginning, from ancient times things which have not been done. Saying my purpose will be established and I will accomplish all my good pleasures. Calling a bird of prey from the east, the man of My purpose from a far country, truly I have spoken, truly I will bring it to pass. I have planned it, surely I will do it" (Isaiah 46:10-11)

Chapter 14: As-Saff (The Rows)

"The scepter shall not depart from Judah, nor the rulers staff from between his feet, until Shiloh comes, and to him shall be the obedience of the peoples" (Genesis 49:10)

"This is the testimony of John, when the Jews sent to him priests and Levites from Jerusalem to ask him, "Who are you?" And he confessed and did not deny, but confessed, "I'm not the Christ." They asked him, "What then? Are you Elijah?" And he said "I am not." "Are you the Prophet?" And he answered, "No." (John 1:19-21)

In Isaiah 3:1-2, it states, For behold, the Lord God of Hosts is going to remove from Jerusalem and Judah both supply and support, the whole supply of bread and the whole supply of water; the mighty man and the warrior, the judge and the prophet…" (Isaiah 3:1-2)

"Behold, My Servant whom I have chosen; My Beloved in whom My soul is well-pleased; I will put My Spirit upon Him, and He shall proclaim justice to the Gentiles" (Matthew 12:18)

These passages taken in totality are very convincing to anyone who is open-minded. The faith of Muslims is reconfirmed when they read such Biblical passages foretelling the coming of Prophet Muhammad. Not only did earlier traditions have prior knowledge of his coming, but they also knew where he would reside. It is for this reason that three Jewish tribes settled in a rural date farming community in the outskirts of Medina. These three tribes were Banu Qainuka'a, Banu Nadhir and Banu Qurayza that settled in Medina a few hundred years prior to the birth of Prophet Muhammad since they knew that he would ultimately reside in Medina. Muslims believe that Prophet Jesus also shared this prophecy with the Jewish people. In John's Gospel the Greek word Paraclete is mentioned which is translated as "the advocate," "comforter," and "teacher."

"When the Helper comes, whom I will send to you from the Father, that is the Spirit of truth who proceeds from the Father, He will testify about me." (John 15:26)

"But when He, the Spirit of truth, comes, He will guide you into all the truth; for He will not speak on His own initiative, but whatever He hears, He will speak; and He will disclose to you what is to come. He will glorify me, for He will take of mine and will disclose it to you." (John 16:13-14)

Muslims believe that the Paraclete is an obvious reference to Prophet Muhammad. However, Christians interpret this verse to mean the coming of the Holy Spirit. It is without doubt that the notion of the Holy Trinity is shrouded in ambiguity and defies logic. Even the most basic assumptions are rarely questioned and accepted as fact. Important questions are not raised. What is the Holy Spirit? Why is God the Father incapable of doing what the Holy Spirit has been created for? Where is it stated in Jesus' own words that the Holy Spirit is a third part of the triune Godhead? How is it that no prophets in either the Old or New Testament knew of the Holy Spirit as being divine and worshipped it? If the Holy Spirit is a source of scripture and God's word, why are there so many gospels and why has there not been any new revelation for nearly 1900 years? How do Christians reconcile the contradictions of Jesus breathing the Holy Spirit in Acts 1 and then stating in John 15:26, "whom I will send to you from the Father?" These are just some of the questions that should be asked by Christians who falsely claim the Holy Spirit as being divine.

When we read the descriptions of what the Comforter is to do, we see that Prophet Muhammad fulfills that characterization. In John 16:13-14, we learn that the Paraclete will testify and glorify Prophet Jesus. The reader should know by now that the Quran gives the highest respect to Prophet Jesus. Recall that in our earlier discussions God has singled out both Prophets Jesus and Moses and placed them in the highest ranks among God's messengers. Thus Muslims, perhaps even more so than Christians, unequivocally and uncompromisingly love Prophet Jesus as well as his mother and his Disciples. It is within the Muslim creed not only to believe in One God and Prophet Muhammad as being the final messenger, but also to believe in earlier prophets and the revelation given to them by God. In other words, one cannot be a Muslim if he or she does not acknowledge that Prophet Jesus was a prophet of God, his miracles, his miraculous birth, and his return. In fact, it is against etiquette to invoke his name without conveying blessings upon him.

Moreover, if we examine more closely the phrase, "he will disclose what is to come," we realize that Prophet Muhammad provided specific information that is not found in any other scripture. There is abundant and detailed information in both the Quran and the Hadiths about the signs of the final hour, what will take place at the time of resurrection and judgment day, descriptions of both heaven and hell, and the measurement of deeds. On the other hand, there is virtually no description of any of these things in the New Testament. If we believe that the Paraclete is the Holy Spirit then we encounter the conundrum that the Holy Spirit did not provide any new disclosure that was not previously known in the Old Testament or the teachings of Prophet Jesus. The only exception is the Book of Revelation, which contains signs of things to come which are quite similar to the Book of Daniel in the Old Testament. Interestingly, it is the angel, according to Revelations 1:1, who provides visions that constitute the Book of Revelation. However, the Book of Revelation was not recognized in early Church ratifications of the canon. The bishops of the fourth and fifth centuries that decided the canon did not want to initially approve an inspired book that was exclusively based on dreams and visions.

If Christians believe the Holy Spirit is the Paraclete who is the third part of the triune Godhead, coeternal, and equal to the Father and the Son, then why does the Holy Spirit not speak for itself? The quote specifically states that "He will not speak on His own initiative, but whatever He hears, He will speak (John 16:13)..." The notion of relying on an external source is inconsistent with the idea of being coequal with God. This attribute of speaking the truth coming from a higher authority is the relationship between God and His messengers. When we take the Paraclete to be Prophet Muhammad, then this verse begins to make complete sense. After all, Prophet Muhammad received the Divine Word from God through the Angel Gabriel. In fact, in the ancient Aramaic text, the word for Paraclete was "Ahmad," then "Munahammana"; this is the Aramaic rendering of the name "Muhammad". Even though the coming of Prophet Muhammad has been well documented in the Bible, the arrival of the Holy Spirit or it being the third part of the triune Godhead is to be found nowhere in the Old Testament.

Verse 14, the last verse that mentions Prophet Jesus, states:

"Believers, be helpers of God, as Jesus Son of Mary said to the disciples, 'Who will be my helpers to God?' The disciples said, 'We will be helpers of God.' And a part of the Israelites believed, while a part scoffed; We backed those who believed against their enemies, so they became

victorious. And God is the almighty, the epitome of wisdom."

This verse is very powerful in that God selects the followers of Prophet Jesus as paragon examples that are worthy of emulation. The level of faith and obedience that the followers of Prophet Jesus showed towards him is the standard that the followers of Prophet Muhammad were expected to uphold. Again, the Biblical version of the Apostles disowning Prophet Jesus and lacking faith is rejected by this Quranic verse, and they in contrast become an embodiment of obedience and piety. Therefore, the notion that the Quran is anti-Jewish should be readily dismissed because the followers of Prophet Jesus were Jewish. God speaks positively of people on the basis of their good faith and actions and not on the grounds of their genealogy or ethnic composition. Like the followers of Prophet Jesus who answered the call to be God's helpers, so too did the companions of Prophet Muhammad. Prophet Muhammad instilled in his followers unwavering faith and moral certitude that contributed to the advent of a glorious Islamic civilization in Baghdad, Spain, and Central and South Asia. While Christendom languished in the Dark Ages, Muslims established a vast civilization that made pioneering advances in mathematics, astronomy, physics, philosophy, biology, chemistry, and the arts.

Part 3
The Trinity and the Crucifixion

15

The Trinity

As has been established thus far, Islam and Christianity are very similar in many ways. There are several areas of commonality between Muslims and Christians. Once again, it is an article of faith for Muslims to believe in Jesus Christ as a great prophet and teacher to mankind. His miraculous birth, his miracles and his return are preserved are in the Quran. This is not true in any other faith, including Judaism. As a result, Muslims and Christians share a special bond that the Quran recognizes in the following passage. In Surah 5 verse 82 it states, **"And you will certainly find the closest of them in affection to the believers are those who say, 'We are Christians.' That is because there are priests and monks among them, and because they are not arrogant."** (5:82).

Despite this recognition, there is an important theological dispute that serves as a source of divide between the two faiths. As readers may be aware by now, the primary difference stems from the Christian conception of the triune God and whether Jesus was truly divine. This chapter will examine the historical development of the Trinity, and Biblical passages will be presented to refute it. We will conclude by discussing the "crucifixion" and "resurrection" of Jesus Christ according to Muslim and Christian perspectives.

The chapters on the Pillars discussed the Islamic conception of God and presented an important excerpt by Imam Ghazali on the subject. The worship of one God is a unifying message that all of the prophets shared. All prophets, including Adam, Abraham, Moses, Jesus, and Prophet Muhammad conveyed this core message to their communities. For instance, on numerous occasions, Jesus Christ is seen prostrating and worshiping that one God. Monotheistic traditions believe that the one true God is all-knowing, all powerful, omnipresent, everlasting, all-seeing, all-hearing, eternal, and the creator and sustainer of the universe. The basic idea of God is virtually identical with the exception of the Christian concept of the Trinity.

Chapter 15: The Trinity

Through the construction of the Trinity, Christians have presented a new and unusual conceptualization of the nature of God that contradicts the Jewish and Muslim notions of oneness. For Muslims, the creation of the Triune God is the single most significant disagreement that produces a deep divide between the two faiths. The notion of the Trinity is a difficult construct to comprehend not only for Jews and Muslims but also for many Christians as well. This is as true today as it was eighteen hundred years ago when it was first introduced. To suggest that God has three different components and yet is one is a source of ambiguity and mystery for most people.

In this discussion of the historical origin and development of the Trinity, we must first keep in mind that the word "trinity" is nowhere to be found in the Old and New Testaments. It first appears in the writings of Theophilus of Antioch in 180 CE. So what was the Christian conceptualization of God prior to the advent of the Trinity during the first two centuries of Christian history?

History recalls that there were myriad opinions on Jesus Christ and how he relates to God. The concept of the Trinity is so complex, even Christian theologians have difficulty explaining how a single God became three. Thus, for our purposes, examining the basic principles may suffice. In the doctrine of the Trinity, God has three distinct parts. More specifically, there is God the Father, God the Son in Jesus Christ, and God the Holy Spirit. These three parts comprise the one Godhead that Christians claim is the Old Testament God, Yahweh.

However, Jews as well as Muslims disagree with such a triune configuration of the one God. In fact, the Ebionites were Jews who accepted Jesus Christ as the messiah and a prophet foretold in the Old Testament. They denied his divinity and considered him as a prophet of God. Similarly, Christian denominations today such as the Jehovah Witnesses also deny Jesus Christ's divinity as it was done when it first took hold. But the strongest movement of Christian believers against the divinity of Jesus Christ was led by a priest named Arius of Alexandria (250-336 CE).

Arius believed since the Logos-Jesus Christ was created by God, hence not eternal, then he cannot be God. He further argued that if the nature or substance of God may be divided or shared by any means, then this would result in the duality of God, which is contrary to the most fundamental Christian belief in the oneness of God. However, Arius was opposed by Athanasius, his superior

Bishop, of Alexandria. Athanasius believed in both Jesus Christ being God but also his worship. As both parties began to openly debate their positions, the battle lines were drawn and the people took to the streets. Consequently, Bishop Athanasius openly denounced Arius and removed him from his priestly position.

As tensions grew between Arius and his growing followers and Athanasius and his supporters, Emperor Constantine, fearing instability, ordered bishops throughout his Empire to meet in Nicea. This was the first of several ecumenical councils that would convene in order to resolve disputes among various Christian churches and the Orthodox, or Catholic, Church. It would also be the first time that a secular party, such as the Emperor, became directly involved let alone presided over Church affairs.

This is crucial in that for over 300 years, the state did not involve itself in the religious affairs of people. This single event changed the course of Christian history. With Emperor Constantine, they had now the support and sponsorship that would legitimatize Christianity at a whole new level, but, as a drawback, Christian doctrine would be guided or directed by the Emperor within his jurisdiction, so as an Emperor died or was overthrown, the Church's doctrine would also change, as the Arian controversy demonstrates.

As ordered by Emperor Constantine, in the year 325 CE, approximately 300 bishops met in Nicea, hence the name The Council of Nicea, in order to unify and decrease rivalry between different Christian churches and their teachings. As talks began on various issues, the greatest source of contention came when the Arian position was heard. Ironically, Arius was not allowed to present his position or sit in the counsel because of his position as a mere priest. Instead, Eusebius of Caesarea, a bishop and a former student of Arius' spoke on behalf of the Arian position. After lengthy and passionate debates, the Arian position was denounced and a formal creed was established. This creed upheld the divinity of Jesus Christ and rejected any notion that he was created and not eternal. This creed, known as the Nicene Creed, states:

> ... Light of light, true God of true God, begotten, not made, of one substance with the Father, through whom all things were made ... (Gonzalez, 1984)

This creed was adopted and signed by the Emperor Constantine and most bishops, with the exception of the bishops who supported the Arian position. However, this did not settle the controversy because a short while later, Eusebius of Caesarea

Chapter 15: The Trinity

approached Emperor Constantine as he was visiting Antioch and restated the Arian position, thereby convincing the Emperor. As a result, Bishop Athanasius was exiled and the Nicean Creed was denounced and their supporters were removed from church positions.

With the change in the official position of the Empire, the Arian movement expanded from the Eastern churches where it had a stronghold and moved into the Western part of the Roman Empire. Thus, most bishops, priests, and laity, in the Christian world believed in the humanity of Jesus Christ. In fact, St. Jerome was quoted as saying, "The whole world groaned and was astonished to find itself Arian." Moreover, they had done so in a matter of decades because when Theodosius I became Emperor in 379 the Empire had a new creed.

As a devout supporter of the Nicene Creed, he ordered bishops to gather in Constantinople, which became the Second Ecumenical Council. The council convened in 381 at Constantinople. This council not only affirmed the Nicene Creed declaring Jesus' divinity, but also the divinity of the Holy Spirit, fermenting the Trinity Doctrine. Moreover, the Emperor removed all Arians from high positions, which they were never able to regain. As a result, their numbers deteriorated over the next few centuries until their conversion to Islam in the seventh century. What is most interesting is that the Arians' conversion to Islam was not difficult, because they were receptive to the Muslim beliefs regarding the humanity of Jesus and not the forced Imperial position of his divinity. In the next section, the Muslim defense of Jesus' humanity and lack of divinity will be articulated using Biblical texts. The following points will be advanced:

1. That Jesus Christ is not divine because he was a created being.

2. That he was not divine because his rank and status was not coequal to God, and

3. Jesus Christ exhibited limitations and dependence which go against the Abrahamic concept of God.

Since John's Gospel is primarily used to authenticate Jesus' divinity, it would be appropriate to begin our discussion with the first verse of this text. John 1:1 states,

"In the beginning was the Word, and the Word was with God,

and the Word was God."

This verse asserts that the Word is God and was with God. This logically means that there are two Gods since reason dictates that one cannot be with another and still speak in the singular. Similarly, if we go by the Christian belief that Jesus Christ sits at the right hand of the Father, we would have to naturally agree that there are two beings, because one cannot sit next to one's self. Therefore, the Logos being God, by its very existence, contradicts the monotheistic belief of the worship of One Almighty God. Furthermore, the fact of Jesus' creation has been well established. Consider the following verses:

"The Lord possessed me at the beginning of His way, before His works of old" (Proverbs 8:22).

"From everlasting I was established, from the beginning, from the earliest times of the earth" (Proverbs 8:23).

These two verses demonstrate that not only was Jesus Christ created, but we learn that it was ostensibly God's first act. The notion that Jesus Christ is divine goes against the truism that God is not created but eternal and self-existing.

Furthermore, the reality that Jesus Christ was created is well documented in the Bible. Consider a few verses on the subject. Colossians 1:15 states,

"He is in the image of the invisible God, the firstborn of all creation."

This verse confirms that Jesus Christ was God's creation and the "firstborn." However, what is most interesting is that Jesus Christ was not God but created in God's image similar to Adam. Certainly, we do not proclaim that Adam was God. Also, in Hebrews 1:6, we note that Jesus Christ is again referred to as the firstborn. It states:

"And when He again brings the firstborn into the world."

Such verses discredit the divinity of Jesus Christ unless Christians concede to the reality that one-third of the Godhead that they worship is a creation.

Now that we have established that Jesus Christ is not eternal but a created being, let us turn to the verses that show that Jesus' rank is not equal to God. Psalms 8:5 states,

Chapter 15: The Trinity

"Yet You have made him little lower then God, and You crown him with glory and majesty!"

From this verse, we correctly identify Jesus Christ's exact position. Although some have claimed that this verse is in reference to Adam, other Bible commentaries have argued that this verse refers to God's first creation, namely Jesus Christ, since he was the first creation. Therefore, Jesus Christ is not God, but his rank is a "little lower." This begs the question, what does a "little lower" mean and where does that put him and what is his actual status with God?

Of the numerous verses of the New Testament that shed light on the precise position of Jesus Christ to God, some powerful and revealing passages have been selected. The first is found in 1st Corinthians 15:28 which states,

"When all things are subjected to Him, then the Son Himself also will be subjected to the One who subjected all things to Him, so that God may be all in all."

This verse illustrates that Jesus Christ will be subjected to God and he will acknowledge his maker and Supreme God. Second, in 1st Corinthians 11:3, Jesus is again regarded as being below the Almighty God and not equal to Him. The verse states,

"But I want you to understand that Christ is the head of every man, and the man is the head of a woman, and God is the head of Christ."

Third, in 1st Timothy 2:5, Paul writes,

"For there is only one God, and one mediator also between God and men, the man Christ Jesus."

This verse places Jesus Christ in a non-authoritative position and a designated mediator. We can conclude that as a mediator he will advocate on behalf of his followers on Judgment Day. But God ultimately is the final authority on the fate of His creation. Interestingly, Muslims also believe that all prophets will try to intercede for their communities on Judgment Day.

John 14:28, states,

"...I go to the Father, for the Father is greater than I."

This verse clearly shows that Jesus Christ acknowledges his own limitations. In fact, in John 13:16, Jesus Christ invokes the slave and master relationship and applies it to himself. It states,

> "Truly, truly, I say to you, a slave is not greater than his master, nor *is* one who is sent greater than the one who sent him."

These are not the words uttered by someone else attributed to Jesus Christ. Rather, these are his personal testimonies in his own words. From the Muslim viewpoint, they are the words uttered by a true prophet of God who recognizes the greatness of God's majesty.

Moreover, a prophet must proclaim his servant status in order that others take notice. We see in Acts 3:13 that Jesus Christ is referred to as a servant by Peter. This verse states,

> "The God of Abraham, Isaac and Jacob, the God of our Fathers, has glorified His servant Jesus, *the one* whom you delivered and disowned in the presence of Pilate, when he had elected to release Him."

For Peter to refer to Jesus Christ as a servant of God *after his ascension* shows that Jesus Christ clearly conveyed his message with regard to his status as no more than a slave and prophet of God. This depiction of Jesus as a servant of God would be incomprehensible today.

As stated earlier, Muslims believe that prophet hood is the highest honor that any being can be bestowed by God. Prophets are the best of God's creations. But even the greatest prophets cannot come infinitely close to the glory, majesty, power, and rank of God. Even though prophets are selected by God, they are mortal human beings completely dependent on God in all aspects of existence. This is certainly true of Jesus Christ as well. The passages below will examine Jesus Christ as a prophet who is dependent on God for guidance and support and possesses human limitations.

To begin, the Christian belief that God became man is an admission of fallibility. Some early Christians had argued that matter is an imperfect state which God would not lower himself to be in. Therefore, a group of Christians accepted Docetism, in which they thought that Jesus Christ did not come in human flesh but appeared that way to people. They believed that he existed in a spiritual

Chapter 15: The Trinity

state which is of a greater existence than human existence. They do have a point to the extent that they sought to resolve that God could not take human form with all the trappings of the human flesh. It is not godlike for the perfect God to become an imperfect being. The God of Abraham, Ishmael, Isaac, Jacob, Prophet Muhammad, and all prophets is invisible and unique. He is without shape or form, and boundaries do not limit His essence. It still remains an egregious sin for anyone to produce an image of God, as it violates the first of God's commandments. Unfortunately, this is what Christians do when they claim Jesus Christ is God incarnate.

Thus far, it has been established that Jesus Christ was a created being and not coequal to God. We will now turn to those passages that demonstrate that he did not possess divine qualities. For example, in Luke 2:52, it states,

> "And Jesus kept increasing in wisdom and stature, and in favor with God and men."

This verse is very important in that it proves that not only did Jesus Christ grow in spirituality, but it brought God pleasure. However, this would change our notion of the Almighty God, because if at any point God is deficient in any way then He no longer is truly divine. In other words, if Jesus Christ lacked or did not possess complete wisdom earlier in his life and obtained it as he grew, then we must concede that he was not divine. The fact is that God is perfect and is beyond increase or diminution. His perfection is so complete that it does not allow for change.

There are numerous examples that show Jesus Christ's lack of omniscience and omnipotence. Such was the case when he felt the power leave him without his knowledge and consent. In Mark 5:24-31, we read that as Jesus Christ was traveling and a crowd was following him, a sick woman decided to touch Jesus Christ's garment in order to be healed. She touched his garment and became cured. More importantly, we learn that Jesus Christ did not know why his power was leaving him or who the woman was. Mark 5:30-31 states,

> "Immediately Jesus, perceiving in himself that the power proceeding from him had gone forth, turned around in the crowd and said, "Who touched my garments?" And His disciples said to Him, "You see the crowd pressing in on you, and you say, 'Who touched me?'"

This is an enlightening passage that reveals Jesus Christ's lack of complete knowledge and control. We learn that Jesus Christ did not know why the power was leaving him or to whom it was going. Moreover, he did not permit it.

In many verses of the New Testament, we see his limitations in knowledge and power. For instance, with regard to the final hour, we read in Matthew 24:36,

> "But of that day and hour no one knows, not even the angels of heaven, nor the Son, but the Father alone."

Jesus Christ in his own words acknowledges his own limitations concerning a vital piece of knowledge. Hence, if he was God or shared in his divinity, then we would expect Jesus Christ to share in God's absolute knowledge and power. Another example of Jesus Christ's lack of omniscience is when he chooses his twelve disciples. When Jesus Christ chose his disciples, he also chose Judas, who later betrays him. Why did he have to make a disciple out of someone as unscrupulous as Judas if he had foreknowledge of his devious nature and the future plot against him? Furthermore, the most surprising of all is what becomes of Judas. Much to my amazement, in Matthew 19:27-28, we read

> "Then Peter said to him, Behold, we have left everything and followed you; what then will there be for us? And Jesus said to them, Truly, I say to you, that you who have followed Me in the regeneration, when the Son of Man will sit on His glorious throne, you also shall sit upon twelve thrones, judging the twelve tribes of Israel."

This verse is very alarming because Judas was included amongst the twelve when Jesus Christ spoke these words. Hence, we can say for certain that Jesus Christ did not have prior knowledge of the Judas conspiracy or he would not have made him a disciple or established a throne for Judas in the "Kingdom" to rule over one of the tribes of Israel.

Another example that shows Jesus Christ's lack of divinity is his lack of omnipotence. We read in Matthew that on the night of Jesus Christ's arrest he repeatedly prayed to God. Matthew 26:39 states,

> "And he went a little beyond *them,* and fell on his face and

prayed, saying, my Father, if it is possible, let this cup pass from me; yet not as I will but as You will.'"

Here, Jesus Christ prays to God in hopes that he may be saved from torment. Although he apparently perceives what lies ahead, he nevertheless prays for his salvation. What drove him to pray is what drives us to pray, fear and helplessness. We see this exact feeling from Jesus Christ. In Matthew 26:38, we read,

"Then he said to them, my soul is deeply grieved, to the point of death: remain here and keep watch with me."

The sense of fear and worry that these words convey is not from a being that can be considered divine. The true God does not fear, worry, grieve, and feel helpless.

Another example of Jesus Christ's lack of omnipotence is in Mark 6:5 which states,

"And He could do no miracle there except that He laid His hands on a few sick people and healed them."

This verse is an excellent example of Jesus Christ not being omnipotent. If he was divine, then there should be no limitations whatsoever on him performing great miracles. One may argue that he could not perform miracles because of the people's lack of faith. Matthew 13:58 states,

"And He did not do many miracles there because of their unbelief."

This is not a legitimate argument for his inability to perform miracles. The entire purpose for performing miracles by prophets is to show that they have indeed been sent by God. A sign from God is meant to bring people of little or no faith to true faith. John 4:48, states,

"So Jesus said to him, Unless you *people* see signs and wonders, you *simply* will not believe."

This verse clarifies for us the actual purpose and effect of miracles. Therefore, peoples' disbelief cannot be the reason why Jesus Christ could do no miracles. Miracles are not performed by prophets but emanate from God. My claim is supported by many passages from the New Testament. The most explicit is found in Acts 2:22 which states,

> "Men of Israel, listen to these words: Jesus the Nazarene, a man attested to you by God with miracles and wonders and signs *which God performed through Him* in your midst, just as you yourselves know."

This is consistent with the Muslim belief that any miracle done by prophets is the work of Almighty God. Concurrently, John 8:28 states,

> "When you lift up the Son of Man, then you will know that I am *He*, and *I do nothing on my own initiative,* but I speak these things as the Father taught me."

We also see many instances in which Jesus Christ looked up into heaven and used God's name to perform miracles. For example, in John 10:25, it states

> "Jesus answered them, I told you, and you do not believe; the works that I do in My Father's name, these testify of *me.*"

This verse confirms that Jesus Christ was not the actual source of the miracles but it was by calling on God. He is repeatedly seen looking up to heaven before performing miracles. For example, Mark 7:34 states,

> "And looking up to heaven with a deep sigh, he said to him, Ephphatha!" that is, 'Be opened' (Mark 7:34)"

Also, Luke 9:16 says,

> "Then He took the five loaves and the two fish, and looking up to heaven, He blessed them…"

These passages provide us with certain details that confirm what Muslims believe about Jesus Christ. Clearly, he performed great miracles by God's will and command. This being said, two additional points need to be made regarding Jesus Christ's miracles.

First, if Christians claim that Jesus Christ is truly God himself, then it becomes rather insignificant to think of miracles as supernatural acts compared to the doings of God. If Jesus is God, then why is the act of raising the dead and

Chapter 15: The Trinity

healing the sick so noteworthy? After all, God is the creator of everything in the heavens and the earth and these are far greater signs of God's majesty and glory. On the other hand, if we see these unexplained phenomena as God's work done through man, then Jesus Christ's acts are true signs and miracles.

Secondly, since Christians argue that Jesus Christ's miracles are proof of his divinity, it should be pointed out that such miracles were performed before as documented in the Old Testament. For example, Jesus Christ was not the only one to raise the dead. In First Kings 17:21-22, Elijah had also brought a dead child back to life.

> "Then he [Elijah] stretched himself upon the child three times, and called to the Lord and said, "O Lord my God, I pray You, let this child's life return to him." The Lord heard the voice of Elijah, and the life of the child returned to him and he revived."

In fact, Elijah's son Elisha also performed this miracle in Second Kings 4:33-34. Even more amazingly, Elisha's dead bones brought life to a dead man. In Second Kings 13:21-22 we read,

> "As they were burying a man, behold, they saw a marauding band; and they cast the man into the grave of Elisha. And when the man touched the bones of Elisha he revived and stood on his feet."

Another of Jesus Christ's miracles that had been previously performed on a lesser scale was the feeding of a large group of people with little available food. We are very familiar with the great miracle of Jesus Christ feeding five thousand people with five loaves and two fish. However, Elisha in Second Kings 4:42-44 states,

> "Now a man came from Baal-shalishah, and brought the man of God bread of the first fruits, twenty loaves of barley and fresh ears of grain in his sack. And he said, 'Give *them* to the people that they may eat.' His attendant said, 'What, will I set this before a hundred men?' But he said, 'Give them to the people that they may eat, for thus says the Lord. They shall eat and have some left over.' So he set *it* before them and they ate and had *some* left over, according to the word of the Lord."

In conclusion, the notion of Jesus' divinity was first disputed by early Christians who referred to themselves as Aryans. This Unitarian position was relatively widespread in the fourth and fifth centuries. Prior to this, there was a wide spectrum of different beliefs on the identity and status of Jesus Christ. It was Constantine the Great who sought to unify these multifarious positions and began to promulgate one accepted conception of Jesus. And as such, the triune conceptualization of God came to be. A closer examination of the four Gospels sheds serious doubt on this triune formulation that emerged as a result of human deliberation at the behest of Constantine. This chapter was devoted to establish that Prophet Jesus was not divine because he exhibited human qualities and limitations. Biblical passages affirm the Muslim position that Jesus Christ was a created being who was sent by God as a prophet to the Children of Israel. As a prophet like several that came before him, he possessed only the knowledge and power that was given to him by God. The next chapter will present the Muslim position on the crucifixion using Biblical passages.

16

The False Crucifixion

Another major difference between Muslims and Christians regarding Jesus Christ is whether he was crucified. Christians believe he died and was buried and ascended into heaven, sitting at the "right hand of the Father." However, Muslims have a different perspective. They believe Jesus Christ did not perish on the cross nor did he die, but God Almighty lifted him into heaven prior to the crucifixion. Although Christians may have difficulty accepting this viewpoint, they should consider the overwhelming evidence that will be presented below.

First, it is not impossible for God to lift up someone into heaven. He had done this repeatedly in the Old Testament. Recall that Elijah in Second Kings 2:11 was lifted up into heaven.

"As they were going along and talking, behold, there appeared a chariot of fire and horse of fire which separated the two of them. And Elijah went up by a whirlwind into heaven."

Moreover, Enoch was lifted up by God in Genesis 5:24 before the flood.

"Enoch walked with God; and he was not, for God took him."

Both Elijah and Enoch are examples of God's mercy and power and that nothing is beyond His purview.

Similarly, according to the teachings of the Catholic Church, Mary was bodily "Assumed" into heaven after her passing. This refers to the belief that she was not buried but her body was raised into heaven. However, there is no Quranic reference that validates this claim. Therefore, Muslims believe that God performed this miracle only with Jesus Christ. This is why Muslims believe that

Jesus Christ will resume his earthly life and, like all human beings, will eventually die and be resurrected on the Day of Judgment.

Furthermore, the Muslim claim that Jesus was not crucified can be authenticated by several Biblical passages. Let us begin with Psalms 20:6.

"Now I know that the Lord saves His anointed; He will answer him from His holy heaven with the saving strength of His right hand."

This verse asserts that God will save "His anointed" with the strength of His right hand. But who is His anointed? If anyone in the Bible can lay claim to being the anointed, we can say without equivocation that it would have to be Jesus Christ. After all, the word Christ literally means "the anointed one."

Also, consider two similar passages. Psalms 41:2 states,

"The Lord will protect him and keep him alive, and he shall be called blessed upon the earth; and do not give him over to the desires of his enemies."

And Psalms 28:8 states,

"The Lord is their strength, and He is a saving defense to His anointed."

These two passages, especially the former, can only refer to Jesus Christ because they are quite clear that God will save and protect the anointed and blessed one. If Jesus Christ was protected and saved from the crucifixion, then we can take the next step in believing that he did not die. It would not make much sense if God's anointed perished and died on the cross if God planned to keep him alive. Assuring the safety and protection of his anointed, God does not give him over to his enemies. The Jewish establishment was the enemy of Jesus Christ, since he threatened their status and authority. But God would not allow their desires to be fulfilled again, since they had murdered prophets in the past. It was for this reason that we read that God on numerous occasions informs Jesus Christ of the Jewish conspiracy to kill him. Soon afterwards, the Bible notes that he successfully escapes from the scene. Thus, God continuously ensures his safety from the beginning. It is reasonable to suggest that God did fulfill His promise and did not allow Jesus Christ to be crucified.

Chapter 16: The False Crucifixion

On the other hand, if we take the Christian position that it was Jesus Christ who perished on the cross, it is difficult to believe that during his last moments he uttered "My God, My God, why has thou forsaken me?" Throughout early Christian history, we are told countless stories of courageous Christians being led to their gruesome death. Yet, they unflinchingly chose to be burned alive in pits of fire rather than denounce the faith and question the will of God. Certainly, such incredulous words questioning God could not be uttered by Jesus Christ who was a beacon of faith.

Additionally, in various verses of the Bible, there were indications that the Messiah was going to be "lifted up." For example, in John 12:32, Jesus Christ said,

> "And I, if I am lifted up from the earth, will draw all men to myself."

And we read in the next verse John's interpretation of the above statement:

> "But He was saying this to indicate the kind of death by which He was to die" (John 12:33).

However, Muslims disagree with John's interpretation of being "lifted up." This phrase captures not the method of his execution but God's rescue of Jesus Christ as foretold in numerous Biblical passages. This claim is supported by the unusual dialogue between Jesus Christ and Satan. According to Matthew 4:6, Satan challenges Jesus Christ by saying:

> "If you are the Son of God, throw yourself down; for it is written, 'He will command His angels concerning you'; and 'On their hands they will bear you up, so that you will not strike your foot against a stone.'"

Ironically, Satan seems to be well versed with the scriptures and makes a reference to Psalms 91:11-12, which states:

> "For He will give His angels charge concerning you, to guard you in your ways, they will bear you up in their hands, that you do not strike your foot against a stone."

These two verses demonstrate that God through his angels would prevent any physical affliction on Jesus Christ. Hence, to test whether Jesus Christ was the true Messiah, Satan dared him to throw himself from the mountain with the recognition that the true Messiah would be saved by God's angels. If we examine both the Psalms and Matthew's account, it becomes clear that angels were entrusted to lift up Jesus Christ so that no harm could come to him. Since angels were assigned this responsibility of protection, we must ask where they were when he was being tortured and crucified.

Although the notion that Jesus Christ died on the cross and redeemed all of the sins of mankind is essentially the basis of all Christian doctrine, the Muslim alternative position is consistent with the above-mentioned scriptures. In essence, Muslims do not find it necessary for "God" to come down as a man and get murdered or sacrificed in order for anyone to enter into heaven. The Muslim position for salvation is based upon God's infinite mercy. This is why God through His prophets taught repentance for their sins. Human beings, unlike other creatures, are endowed with free will and have the choice to accept or reject faith. Thus, sin is the byproduct of being human. Sin also enables humans to recognize their own imperfections, and as such, their need for God who is the embodiment of perfection. Through repentance, humans are coming to God asking for His forgiveness. This is why repentance is the key to salvation. In the Old Testament, repentance and forgiveness appear hundreds of times while in the New Testament, these two words appear fifty-two times.

Moreover, in Christianity, the greatest sin that a person can commit is a sin against the Holy Spirit. To proclaim that any sin is so great so as to not be forgivable by the Holy Spirit is considered to be a sin against the Holy Spirit itself. In other words, the Holy Spirit is seen as so merciful that it can forgive all sins. Why, then, does it become necessary for God to come down as a man and be sacrificed if humans can repent for themselves?

It is also inconsistent that, according to the Bible, the original sin of Prophet Adam is somehow not foreseen by God and beyond His control. This is what we are told in Genesis 3:22,

> "Then the Lord God said, Behold, the man has become like one of Us, knowing good and evil; and now, he might stretch out his hand and take also from the tree of life, and eat and live forever."

This verse teaches that God was not able to prevent Adam from learning

Chapter 16: The False Crucifixion

about good and evil or living forever like God Himself. Hence, in Genesis 6:6 God is regretful of the creation of Adam.

> "The Lord was sorry that He had made man on the earth, and He was grieved in His heart."

Such constructs are inconsistent with the concept of an all-knowing and all-powerful One True God. Muslims believe Prophet Adam's actions were absolutely consistent with God's plan. Prior to the formation of the universe, God had created the human race in its initial spiritual state, having full knowledge that they would be conceived through Adam and Eve. God created Adam and gave him knowledge and free will and then tested him. God also knew that Adam would be tricked by Satan and eat from the forbidden tree. Through Adam's sin, we are able to come into our earthly existence with free will to worship or reject God. This is the purpose of the Day of Judgment so that God can determine who will be granted paradise by their faith and good deeds, and who will be damned by their rebellion and bad actions. God's mercy and justice require that He bestow the gift of heaven to those who have faith in Him and do righteous deeds.

Conversely, the Christian belief that original sin is inherited and the cause of damnation for humankind is problematic, to say the least. Our basic understanding of the principles of true justice dictate an individual cannot be held accountable and punished for the actions of others. As such, this principle is clearly stated in both the Quran and the Bible. This first appears in Ezekiel 18:20 which states:

> "The person who sins will die. The son will not bear the punishment for the father's iniquity, nor will the father bear the punishment for the son's iniquity; the righteousness of the righteous will be upon himself, and the wickedness of the wicked will be upon himself."

This is later affirmed in Surah 2:134 which states:

> **"That was a people that hath passed away. They shall reap the fruit of what they did, and ye of what ye do! Of their merits there is no question in your case!"**

Therefore, Muslims categorically reject the Christian notion that the children of Adam will be punished for the sins of their original parents- sins for which they have already been forgiven. **"Our Lord! We have wronged our own souls: If thou forgive us not and bestow not upon us Thy Mercy, we shall certainly be lost."**

In short, the keys to salvation include faith, observance of holy laws, goodness to creation, and repentance. This is what Prophet Jesus Christ, along with other messengers of God, taught their people.

Epilogue

In conclusion, we began our discussion on Islam with Prophet Abraham, as was appropriate. I presented passages demonstrating that Arabs are the descendants of Abraham, and Muslims are the followers of his grandson, Prophet Muhammad. Thus, Muslims, Christians, and Jews have not only shared a familial bond, but also are the only people that proclaim the monotheistic tradition.

We have been given the scriptures that teach us the oneness of God, the belief in angels, the resurrection, heaven, hell, the Day of Judgment, and so forth. These organized systems of belief separate us from other faiths. It is absolutely imperative that we recognize this truth and, at the same time, respect our differences. The sole objective of this book was to inform my cousins in faith – the Christians – who Muslims are and what we truly believe. In answering this question, Prophet Jesus became our main focus, since both Christians and Muslims believe that he was the true Messiah. I used the Holy Quran as a main source to illuminate the Muslim perspective regarding this great prophet. I discussed in detail various Quranic references that directly identify Prophet Jesus. Through textual analysis, the reader knows precisely what Muslims believe about him.

Muslims as well as Christians share in the belief that Jesus Christ was a prophet and servant of God. By the word of God he was made flesh, born to a virgin, performed numerous miracles, and preached the Gospel and the Commandments. We also find commonality in the belief that he worshipped and prayed to his Lord; he was lifted into heaven and will return in a similar manner to be a mediator on the Day of Judgment. All of these beliefs have been well-documented in both the Quran and the Bible. Furthermore, by examining the passages that mention Prophet Jesus, we may identify the more significant differences between Muslims and Christians. For example, Muslims reject Prophet Jesus' divinity and his status as the Son of God, nor do Muslims believe he was crucified and died on the cross; God was not sacrificed for the sins of humankind. Muslims also reject the trinity doctrine, believing instead that the Holy Spirit was the Angel Gabriel.

These beliefs are well-corroborated in the Bible and early church history. Despite my thorough argument in favor of the Muslim positions, it is not intended to persuade Christians to abandon their beliefs. Rather, I hope Christians begin a critical study of what they believe; research for yourself when and how a particular dogma was assimilated into mainstream Christianity. After such an examination, your Christian faith may or may not be validated. In either case, your faith will be based upon knowledge as opposed to ignorance. This is not to say that either Christians or Muslims can rightly proclaim that they alone are the possessors of the truth. More important is to respect one another while disagreeing with sincerity. After all, these beliefs are matters of faith. The Quran states in Surah 2:256, **"There is no compulsion in religion,"** meaning that Muslims are prohibited from imposing their faith on non-believers. This is contrary to the popular opinions of Islam as shared in the West. To further establish this Muslim teaching, there is an entire Surah devoted to the virtue of pluralism. There is an entire chapter exclusively devoted to this truth. In Surah 109, titled, "Unbelievers," it is stated, **"Say, 'O [unbelievers], I don't serve what you serve, and you don't serve what I serve, and I won't serve what you serve, and you won't serve what I serve, you have your way, and I have my way.'"**

Although that Surah was revealed in Mecca, its message and principles apply with equal felicity today. The respect for the faith of another is paramount for the peace and security of the world. We must recognize that the global village has diverse people and numerous faiths, deserving of our respect and tolerance. We are all one human family and children of Adam and Eve. **"O humankind, We created you from a male and a female, and We made you races and tribes for you to get to know each other. The most noble of you in the sight of God are those of you who are most conscientious. And God is omniscient, fully aware."** (Surah 49:13)

If God had desired to create human beings under only one religion and removed the capacity for sin, he could have done so. By giving human beings the freedom to choose their own faith without any compulsion, God establishes the Day of Judgment. In other words, the purpose of Judgment is based upon the free will – choosing between good or bad, faith or unbelief, righteousness or wickedness. As such, the responsibility and the accountability is within each person. In the end, God will decide the weight of our faith and actions; it is not our right as humans to act as judges, preaching damnation for others and boasting salvation for themselves. We must be able to openly discuss our similarities and

Epilogue

humbly examine our differences. Engaging in civil discourse brings us to a greater understanding and leads to the removal of prejudice and hatred.

Muslims and Christians comprise more than one half of the world's population. Hence together, we could become the instruments of peace, justice and equality espoused by Prophet Jesus and Prophet Muhammad- may God's peace and blessings be upon them both.

Appendix

PROPHET MUHAMMAD'S FAREWELL SERMON

Date delivered: 632 A.C., 9th day of Dhul-Hijjah, 10 A.H. in the 'Uranah valley of Mount Arafat.

After praising, and thanking God, he said: "O People, listen well to my words, for I do not know whether, after this year, I shall ever be amongst you again. Therefore listen to what I am saying to you very carefully and TAKE THESE WORDS TO THOSE WHO COULD NOT BE PRESENT HERE TODAY.

O People, just as you regard this month, this day, and this city as Sacred, so regard the life and property of every Muslim as a sacred trust. Return the goods entrusted to you to their rightful owners. Treat others justly so that no one would be unjust to you. Remember that you will indeed meet your LORD, and that HE will indeed reckon your deeds. God has forbidden you to take usury (riba), therefore all riba obligation shall henceforth be waived. Your capital, however, is yours to keep. You will neither inflict nor suffer inequity. God has judged that there shall be no riba and that all the riba due to `Abbas ibn `Abd al Muttalib shall henceforth be waived.

Every right arising out of homicide in pre-Islamic days is henceforth waived and the first such right that I waive is that arising from the murder of Rabi`ah ibn al Harith ibn `Abd al Muttalib.

O Men, the Unbelievers indulge in tampering with the calendar in order to make permissible that which God forbade, and to forbid that which God has made permissible. With God the months are twelve in number. Four of them are sacred, three of these are successive and one occurs singly between the months of Jumada and Sha`ban. Beware of the devil, for the safety of your religion. He has

Appendix

lost all hope that he will ever be able to lead you astray in big things, so beware of following him in small things.

O People, it is true that you have certain rights over your women, but they also have rights over you. Remember that you have taken them as your wives only under God's trust and with His permission. If they abide by your right then to them belongs the right to be fed and clothed in kindness. Treat your women well and be kind to them, for they are your partners and committed helpers. It is your right and they do not make friends with anyone of whom you do not approve, as well as never to be unchaste...

O People, listen to me in earnest, worship God (The One Creator of the Universe), perform your five daily prayers (Salah), fast during the month of Ramadan, and give your financial obligation (zakah) of your wealth. Perform Hajj if you can afford to.

All mankind is from Adam and Eve, an Arab has no superiority over a non-Arab nor a non-Arab has any superiority over an Arab; also a white has no superiority over a black nor a black has any superiority over white except by piety and good action. Learn that every Muslim is a brother to every Muslim and that the Muslims constitute one brotherhood. Nothing shall be legitimate to a Muslim which belongs to a fellow Muslim unless it was given freely and willingly. Do not, therefore, do injustice to yourselves.

Remember, one day you will appear before God (The Creator) and you will answer for your deeds. So beware, do not stray from the path of righteousness after I am gone.

O People, NO PROPHET OR APOSTLE WILL COME AFTER ME AND NO NEW FAITH WILL BE BORN. Reason well, therefore, O People, and understand words which I convey to you. I leave behind me two things, the QURAN and my example, the SUNNAH and if you follow these you will never go astray.

All those who listen to me shall pass on my words to others and those to others again; and may the last ones understand my words better than those who listen to me directly. Be my witness, O GOD, that I have conveyed your message to your people".

THE CHARTER OF MEDINA

Full Text of the Medina Charter: The first written constitution in the history of the world documented by Prophet Muhammad (PBUH) after His migration to Medina and establishment of the first Islamic community and city-state.

1. This is a document from Muhammad the Prophet (may God bless him and grant him peace), governing relations between the Believers i.e. Muslims of Quraysh and Yathrib and those who followed them and worked hard with them. They form one nation -- Ummah.
2. The Quraysh Mohajireen will continue to pay blood money, according to their present custom.
3. In case of war with anybody they will redeem their prisoners with kindness and justice common among Believers. (Not according to pre-Islamic nations where the rich and the poor were treated differently).
4. The Bani Awf will decide the blood money, within themselves, according to their existing custom.
5. In case of war with anybody all parties other than Muslims will redeem their prisoners with kindness and justice according to practice among Believers and not in accordance with pre-Islamic notions.
6. The Bani Saeeda, the Bani Harith, the Bani Jusham and the Bani Najjar will be governed on the lines of the above (principles)
7. The Bani Amr, Bani Awf, Bani Al-Nabeet, and Bani Al-Aws will be governed in the same manner.
8. Believers will not fail to redeem their prisoners they will pay blood money on their behalf. It will be a common responsibility of the Ummah and not of the family of the prisoners to pay blood money.
9. A Believer will not make the freedman of another Believer as his ally against the wishes of the other Believers.
10. The Believers, who fear God, will oppose the rebellious elements and those that encourage injustice or sin, or enmity or corruption among Believers.
11. If anyone is guilty of any such act all the Believers will oppose him even if he be the son of any one of them.
12. A Believer will not kill another Believer, for the sake of an un-Believer. (i.e. even though the un-Believer is his close relative).
13. No Believer will help an un-Believer against a Believer.

Appendix

14. Protection (when given) in the Name of God will be common. The weakest among Believers may give protection (In the Name of God) and it will be binding on all Believers.
15. Believers are all friends to each other to the exclusion of all others.
16. Those Jews who follow the Believers will be helped and will be treated with equality. (Social, legal and economic equality is promised to all loyal citizens of the State).
17. No Jew will be wronged for being a Jew.
18. The enemies of the Jews who follow us will not be helped.
19. The peace of the Believers (of the State of Medina) cannot be divided. (it is either peace or war for all. It cannot be that a part of the population is at war with the outsiders and a part is at peace).
20. No separate peace will be made by anyone in Medina when Believers are fighting in the Path of God.
21. Conditions of peace and war and the accompanying ease or hardships must be fair and equitable to all citizens alike.
22. When going out on expeditions a rider must take his fellow member of the Army-share his ride.
23. The Believers must avenge the blood of one another when fighting in the Path of God (This clause was to remind those in front of whom there may be less severe fighting that the cause was common to all. This also meant that although each battle appeared a separate entity it was in fact a part of the War, which affected all Muslims equally).
24. The Believers (because they fear God) are better in showing steadfastness and as a result receive guidance from God in this respect. Others must also aspire to come up to the same standard of steadfastness.
25. No un-Believer will be permitted to take the property of the Quraysh (the enemy) under his protection. Enemy property must be surrendered to the State.
26. No un-Believer will intervene in favor of a Quraysh, (because the Quraysh having declared war are the enemy).
27. If any un-believer kills a Believer, without good cause, he shall be killed in return, unless the next of kin are satisfied (as it creates law and order problems and weakens the defense of the State). All Believers shall be against such a wrong-doer. No Believer will be allowed to shelter such a man.
28. When you differ on anything (regarding this Document) the matter shall be referred to God and Muhammad (may God bless him and grant him peace).
29. The Jews will contribute towards the war when fighting alongside the Believers.

30. The Jews of Bani Awf will be treated as one community with the Believers. The Jews have their religion. This will also apply to their freedmen. The exception will be those who act unjustly and sinfully. By so doing they wrong themselves and their families.
31. The same applies to Jews of Bani Al-Najjar, Bani Al Harith, Bani Saeeda, Bani Jusham, Bani Al Aws, Thaalba, and the Jaffna, (a clan of the Bani Thaalba) and the Bani Al Shutayba.
32. Loyalty gives protection against treachery. (loyal people are protected by their friends against treachery. As long as a person remains loyal to the State he is not likely to succumb to the ideas of being treacherous. He protects himself against weakness).
33. The freedmen of Thaalba will be afforded the same status as Thaalba themselves. This status is for fair dealings and full justice as a right and equal responsibility for military service.
34. Those in alliance with the Jews will be given the same treatment as the Jews.
35. No one (no tribe which is party to the Pact) shall go to war except with the permission of Muhammad (may God bless him and grant him peace). If any wrong has been done to any person or party it may be avenged.
36. Anyone who kills another without warning (there being no just cause for it) amounts to his slaying himself and his household, unless the killing was done due to a wrong being done to him.
37. The Jews must bear their own expenses (in War) and the Muslims bear their expenses.
38. If anyone attacks anyone who is a party to this Pact the other must come to his help.
39. They (parties to this Pact) must seek mutual advice and consultation.
40. Loyalty gives protection against treachery. Those who avoid mutual consultation do so because of lack of sincerity and loyalty.
41. A man will not be made liable for misdeeds of his ally.
42. Anyone (any individual or party) who is wronged must be helped.
43. The Jews must pay (for war) with the Muslims. (This clause appears to be for occasions when Jews are not taking part in the war. Clause 37 deals with occasions when they are taking part in war).
44. Yathrib will be Sanctuary for the people of this Pact.
45. A stranger (individual) who has been given protection (by anyone party to this Pact) will be treated as his host (who has given him protection) while (he is) doing no harm and is not committing any crime. Those given protection but indulging in anti-state activities will be liable to punishment.

Appendix

46. A woman will be given protection only with the consent of her family (Guardian). (A good precaution to avoid inter-tribal conflicts).
47. In case of any dispute or controversy, which may result in trouble the matter must be referred to God and Muhammad (may God bless him and grant him peace), The Prophet (may God bless him and grant him peace) of God will accept anything in this document, which is for (bringing about) piety and goodness.
48. Quraysh and their allies will not be given protection.
49. The parties to this Pact are bound to help each other in the event of an attack on Yathrib.
50. If they (the parties to the Pact other than the Muslims) are called upon to make and maintain peace (within the State) they must do so. If a similar demand (of making and maintaining peace) is made on the Muslims, it must be carried out, except when the Muslims are already engaged in a war in the Path of God. (So that no secret ally of the enemy can aid the enemy by calling upon Muslims to end hostilities under this clause).
51. Everyone (individual) will have his share (of treatment) in accordance with what party he belongs to. Individuals must benefit or suffer for the good or bad deed of the group they belong to. Without such a rule party affiliations and discipline cannot be maintained.
52. The Jews of al-Aws, including their freedmen, have the same standing, as other parties to the Pact, as long as they are loyal to the Pact. Loyalty is a protection against treachery.
53. Anyone who acts loyally or otherwise does it for his own good (or loss).
54. God approves this Document.
55. This document will not (be employed to) protect one who is unjust or commits a crime (against other parties of the Pact).
56. Whether an individual goes out to fight (in accordance with the terms of this Pact) or remains in his home, he will be safe unless he has committed a crime or is a sinner. (I.e. No one will be punished in his individual capacity for not having gone out to fight in accordance with the terms of this Pact).
57. God is the Protector of the good people and those who fear God, and Muhammad (may God bless him and grant him peace) is the Messenger of God (He guarantees protection for those who are good and fear God).

POPULATION COMPARISON TABLES

Country	% of Christian Citizens
Lebanon	39%
Egypt	10%
Jordan	6%
Sudan	5%
Iraq	3%

Country	% of Muslim Citizens
EUROPE	
France	5% - 10%
Germany	3.7%
England	2.7%
Canada	1.9%
USA	0.6%

Source: CIA – The World Factbook

Appendix

Works Cited

Ali, Abdullah Yusuf. *The Holy Quran : English Translation By Abdullah Yusuf Ali*. New Delhi: Goodword Books, 2003. Print.

"CIA - The World Factbook." *Central Intelligence Agency*. United States Government, n.d. Web. 4 Nov. 2009. <https://www.cia.gov/library/publications/the-world-factbook/geos/us.html>.

Cleary, Thomas. *The Qur'an: A New Translation*. NY: Starlatch, Llc, 2004. Print.

Friedman, M., Lawrence. "A Dead Language: Divorce Law and Practice Before No-Fault." *Virginia Law Review Association* 86 (2000). Print.

Ghazali, Al. *The Revival of Religious Sciences*. City Unknown: Sufi Publishing Co, 1972. Print.

Gonzalez, Justo L.. *The Story of Christianity: Volume 1: Volume One: The Early Church to the Reformation (Story of Christianity)*. San Francisco: Harper San Francisco, 1984. Print.

Greeley, Andrew. "The Demand for Religion: Hard Core Atheism and 'Supply Side' Theory." University of Chicago. <http://www.agreeley.com/articles/hardcore.html>.

Haleem, M. A. S. Abdel. *The Qur'an (Oxford World's Classics)*. New York: Oxford University Press, USA, 2005. Print.

Lings, Martin. *Muhammad: His Life Based on the Earliest Sources*. New York: Inner Traditions, 2006. Print.

"Pew Forum: Global Muslim Population: Executive Summary." *Pew Forum on Religion & Public Life*. N.p., n.d. Web. 16 Nov. 2009. <http://pewforum.org/docs/?DocID=450>.

Posner, Sarah. *God's Profits: Faith, Fraud, and the Republican Crusade for Values Voters*. Chicago: Polipoint Press, 2008. Print.

Ross, Brian. ABC News. McCain Pastor: Islam Is a 'Conspiracy of Spiritual Evil' 22 May 2008. <http://abcnews.go.com/Blotter/story?id=4905624>.

Schopenhauer, Arthur. *On women*. City Unknown: Felshin, 1931. Print.

New American Standard Bible. Anaheim: Foundation Publications, 1997. Print.

Suggested Readings

These and other titles are available at Furqaanbookstore.com

The Clear Quran – A Thematic English Translation of the Message of the Final Revelation
   Translation by Dr. Mustafa Khattab
The Emergence of Islam
   by Muhammad Hamidullah and Afzal Iqbal
Even Angels Ask: A Journey to Islam in America
   by Jeffrey Lang
The Heart of Islam: Enduring Values for Humanity
   by Seyyed Hossein Nasr
Introduction to Islam
   by Muhammad Hamidullah
Islamic Roots of Democratic Pluralism
   by Abdulaziz Sachedina
Jesus: prophet of Islam
   by Muhammad Ata-ur Rahim
Misquoting Jesus: The Story Behind Who Changed the Bible and Why
   by Bart D. Ehrman
Muhammad: His Life Based on the Earliest Sourcse
   by Martin Lings
The Mythmaker: Paul and the Invention of Christianity
   by Hyam Maccoby
The Quran, Bible, and Science
   by Maurice Bucaille
The Sealed Nectar: Biography of the Noble Prophet
   by Safi-ur-Rahman al Mubarkpuri
Struggling to Surrender: Some Impressions of an American Convert to Islam
   by Jeffrey Lang
What Did Jesus Really Say
   by Abdullah bin Mish'aal

ABOUT THE AUTHOR

The book at your hand is the result of seven years of strenuous research and study by Adil Nizamuddin Imran. A teacher in profession, he holds a Masters in Counseling and has been focusing his scholarship as well as people-skills on topics that will promote faith, tolerance and mutual understanding in our multi-cultural society.

He can be reached through the publisher at christjesus@bookofsigns.org